COLD CALLING

IS LIKE A **COLONOSCOPY**

WITHOUT THE DRUGS

How You Can Find New Business
with Courage, Cold Calling and a Few Less
Invasive Techniques

Jerry Hocutt

Chugwater Publishing

For information about special discounts for bulk purchases, please contact Jerry Hocutt at jerry.ht@footinthedoor.com

First printing 2015

Hocutt, Jerry
    Cold Calling Is Like a Colonoscopy without the Drugs: How You Can Find New Business with Courage, Cold Calling and a Few Less Invasive Techniques
1st edition.

ISBN 978-0692493106
Library of Congress Control Number 2015910264
    1. Sales. 2. Business. 3. Marketing. 4. Management. II. Hocutt, Jr., Jerry E.
    III. Title

Cover design by Jana Hocutt Lacroix

To Linda

When I was young I was always thinking, "Should I say that?" Now that I'm older I say, "What the hell, let's see what happens."

– Unknown (but my money's on Mom)

Contents

Introduction

Cold calling, like a colonoscopy, is a pain in the butt. You may not like the process, but they can both save your ass.

My objective with this book is direct: to help you find new business by *getting you in front of the people who can buy*.

I've been a student all my life for how to get in front of buyers. There is no one answer. There are many answers. I'm curious. I'm always experimenting with new ideas. Some things work. Some don't. I make a lot of mistakes. I trip over myself. I get egg on my face. That's the price for being human and dealing with humans.

Life, selling, cold calling – it's a messy business. A scary business. That's what makes it exciting. Besides, who can ever be bored when you're scared?

What you'll get from this book is what you can't get from anywhere else: my perspective. You'll learn what I've learned up until now. It just won't take you a lifetime to learn it like it did me.

Part one of this book is about the mental game of cold calling: how to get the courage to deal with your fears to do *whatever it takes* to get in front of buyers. Part two includes specific strategies and techniques to get there. And not all have anything to do with cold calling as you know it.

Cold calling is 95% mental, 5% physical. If you can speak, dial a phone, leave a voicemail, knock on doors, network, work a trade show, or send an email, then you can cold call. But it takes courage to take that first step. Courage is the elephant in the room that no one talks about when it comes to selling.

I started to get serious about cold calling when I was ten years old. I'd make pot holders and ride my bike through neighborhoods, knocking on doors and asking the ladies of the house if they'd like to buy "two for a quarter". I went door-to-door selling Boy Scout candies at age eleven. I started my own lawn mowing business in the hot Texas summers by knocking on doors at the age of twelve. These were the years when I first learned how scary cold calling can be. But over time I found how to get the courage to keep knocking on those doors. It works. You'll see.

I've shared my techniques with the thousands of salespeople, executives, managers, entrepreneurs, professionals, principals, business owners, Ivy League professors – even the U.S. Marines – who have attended my seminars. The techniques work for them, and they'll work for you.

As the title of the book indicates, I like to have fun in my job and try not to take myself too seriously. My work, yes. Myself, no. Once you start reading, I think you'll agree that fun is not only one of our best motivators, but it can give you the courage to act as well.

Part One

Courage

1

The Answer Is Sex

The question: How are babies made?

Answer: You have runners on base.

Question: How do you score runs in baseball? (Oakland A's general manager Billie Beane.)

Answer: Keep your mouth shut.

Question: How do you lose weight?

Answer: Courage.

Question: What do you need to find new customers?

The questions are easy. The answers are simple and true. Making it happen is the problem. (Except for the first one!)

> *courage, n. The ability to do something that*
> *you know is difficult or dangerous.*
> Merriam-Webster

Selling takes courage not because it's dangerous, but because it's difficult. It takes courage to cold call, network, ask for referrals, cross-sell, handle objections, call a demanding customer to break the bad news, negotiate, and ask for the business.

Part one of this book is about how to get the courage it takes to get in front of customers who can buy your services and products. The bad news: courage isn't a skill that you can learn like hitting a tennis ball or driving a car. The good – no great! – news: courage comes with the first step.

Read that last sentence again. It may be the most important one in the book.

The mystery of where courage comes from is so simple and straightforward that you may refuse to believe it. You're thinking it has to be more complicated than that. It's not.

Courage comes with the first step! Not a second before. Not a second too late. Courage is a test of your faith. Your actions bear witness to your faith.

There is a memorable scene in the movie *Indiana Jones and the Last Crusade* where Jones is standing on the precipice of a cliff with a bottomless chasm separating him from the other side where the Holy Grail is sitting. His faith tells him that if he would just step into the void a footbridge would appear and carry him safely to the other side. Holding his breath with a prayer he takes the first step. The bridge appears. He makes it safely to the other side.

Think back to the times when you had butterflies before a scary situation. Maybe it was a job interview. Giving a speech. Cold calling. Asking for the order.

Remember what happened once you started? Nothing. The butterflies fluttered off and you did fine. You were probably thinking to yourself as you were talking, "This is easy. Wait a minute, this is crazy. I'm talking to myself as I'm talking with someone else. What's going on?"

After finishing you said, "I don't know what I was so worried about. That went fine."

Courage is the ability to do something that you know is difficult.

But what if you can make that something less difficult?

We'll explore how to make your work less difficult by giving you ways to make that first step easier; by using fun to lower the stress; by practicing the skills it takes to increase your confidence; and by focusing on the process of what you're doing instead of being obsessed about the results.

2

Scalpel!

"I could sell to anybody...if I could just get in front of them first."

Dissect that sentence and see if you can learn what the speaker is really saying. It's not complicated. Pretty obvious.

I'll wait.

Nothing?

Okay. How about this: "I could sell to anybody" because I'm persuasive, talented, and charming. Did I mention good looking? Just ask my friends. (Keep my family out of this!)

Keep cutting down to the bone: "...if I could just get in front of them first." If I just had the *courage to do what it takes* to get in front of them; which I don't. Therefore, I can't sell to anybody after all and will have to wait for them to find and contact me. Hope I'm still in my job when they call.

Jon, my first GM, was famous for regularly tearing through our sales room ranting and raving at the salespeople who were sitting around BS-ing. "What are you doing in the office? Get out of here! Hit the streets! Find some customers! Quit sitting around the office waiting for the phone to ring!"

It's easy to find customers. Look on the internet. There are thousands buying what you sell. Hundreds probably buying today even.

Getting in front of them? That's the trick. I've been in, sat in, and witnessed hundreds of sales meetings where the discussions centered around how to find more new business.

I can count on one hand (minus four fingers) the number of managers who have been upfront with the salespeople about the sales elephant in the room: it takes *courage* to get in front of customers.*

Consider yourself told.

---

*My billionaire boss was the only one who saw the elephant in the room. For years, every "want ad" he ran looking for salespeople or that he gave to staffing agencies had the same first six words: "Must be willing to cold call."

I asked him why he insisted that those be the first words. He said, "It eliminates most people. I'm not looking for salespeople. Most people can sell. I'm looking for people who will do what it takes to get in front of customers who can buy."

He was looking for people with courage. Guess that's why he's a billionaire?

3

If Your Job Doesn't Scare You, Find One That Will

To feel really alive, to avoid the boredom that comes with so many jobs, you need to find work that will test you – even scare you. Who wants to ride a roller coaster on a flat track in a circle? You search out for Diablo's revenge: the meanest, scariest, cruelest ride devised by the Devil himself. Remember the exhilaration, laughter, and excitement you experienced when getting off?

It took courage to make the decision to ride. Courage to get strapped in. And courage on that first steep eighty-foot climb to the top. But you'll remember that ride forever.

And that's why it's important to have work that challenges you to take risks. Your work pulls the courage out of you that you never knew you had.

*Don't look for courage. It can't be
found. Instead, act. Courage will find
you.*

— Jerry Hocutt

Soldiers who go into combat know they're going into dangerous situations. That's courage. Firefighters rushing into burning buildings know their lives are at risk. It takes courage. A policeman chasing an armed suspect into a dark alley goes in with courage.

Courage can be a fifth grader getting in front of the class to tell what he did over the summer. An athlete nervously waiting for the game to begin. Courage can be leaving home for the first time.

You weren't hired to sell because of your courage. There was no checkbox in the job description for courage. You didn't include the word courage anywhere in your résumé. No, you were hired to do a job, to sell. Maybe it was assumed you have the courage. (Maybe now someone should have asked? Just saying.)

Anyway, you're here. You're in sales. Don't make it hard on yourself. Mastering your skills will make selling easier. Like a magician, practice your skills until you reach the level of being "unconsciously competent": no thought is required, everything is a habit, you know without even knowing how you know. Like a magician, you want to leave people in awe and wondering "How did you do that?"

*skill, n. The ability to do something that
comes from training, experience, or
practice.*

— Merriam-Webster

Selling, like any profession, is a nuanced business. It's the small things, the tiny things you do that set you apart. What did her handshake mean? He's curt and short on the phone. What does that tell me? How do I get the nervousness out of my voice? Mastering the small, basic skills will make a difference in your confidence and performance.

Soldiers decorated for heroism in combat all say the same thing: "I was scared to death. But my training kicked in and I did what I had to do." They weren't trying to be courageous. They were doing the job they were trained for. Training makes your job less difficult and makes your decisions better, quicker and faster.

What are the sales skills you need to get in front of more customers? Can you make the difficult less difficult? Is it hard? Can it be fun? Many. Yes. No. Yes.

Let's get on the roller coaster and see what happens. It'll be fun. I guarantee it.

4

Your Job Depends on Your Answer to This Question – Don't Screw It Up

You can use this to…

1. Ask tough questions of yourself to find your own answers.
2. Be persistent and never give up.
3. Learn how to ask good questions so that every phase in the selling process gets easier and better, from negotiating to handling objections to qualifying prospects to closing sales.

Cornered by Paul, my Fortune 1000 sales manager, after our last sales meeting in December (after being on the job for only six weeks), he asked me the best sales question ever: "Why can't you sell? Why can't we sell?" Translation: *"Why can't you get in front of more customers?"*

I knew my job was on the line. Everyone's was; mine, my sales manager's, everyone. No one had been meeting quota for months. Our company had been undergoing a tumultuous overhaul in the six months before I came on board. The turnover rate of our branch's twenty-five person salesforce was over 90%. No one—management or salespeople—had the answer to Paul's question.

Of course, I had the proper response: "Look Paul, if I knew don't you think I'd be doing it? Don't you think you would?" Then I turned and walked away. It's a wonder he didn't fire me for such a smart-ass comeback.

One week later, driving in to work after the New Year's, a picture flashed through my mind. I knew immediately that was the answer to Paul's question. I knew why I couldn't get in front of buying customers.

I fleshed out the answer as I finished driving in to work. My answer created more questions. Those questions had easier answers. Everything fell into place.

My general manager later noticed that my sales turned that very day. I would become the company's number one salesperson in the nation for three years. My managers had me show the answer to the other salespeople. Everyone's sales dramatically improved within two months. We became the number one branch for our company every year.

What was the answer? I'll tell you in the next chapter. But for you, that answer may not be important. It may not be the answer you're looking for. Every situation, every salesperson is different.

What is important is Paul's question "Why can't you sell?" Why can't you get in front of more customers? The question became a "pebble in my shoe"; an irritant that wouldn't let me rest. He asked me that question thirty years ago. It's still a relevant question for every salesperson and manager today. Asking good questions is an art.

If you want to learn how to ask better questions, check out Philip Mudd's book *The HEAD Game: High Efficiency Analytic Decision-Making and the Art of Solving Complex Problems Quickly*. Mudd is a former deputy director of the CIA Counterterrorist Center and FBI National Security Branch. It will help you in cold calling, negotiating, qualifying prospects, interviewing, and solving problems you face in business today. His premise: asking the right questions leads to unexpected discoveries that lead to better decisions.

Paul's question not only taught me the importance of asking the right questions, but that you should never stop looking for the answer. The answers are there. They're just waiting for the right questions. Cancer will someday be cured when someone asks the right question.

Like Paul, you don't need to have all the answers. By asking the right question you may help the other person come up with the answer *they're* looking for on their own. And they'll give you the credit for being so perceptive.

5

Every Boss Wants Their Own SEAL Team 6

You can use this to…
1. Change your thinking and give yourself reasons to get in front of more customers.
2. Use beliefs to create courage.

Why can't you get the courage to get in front of more customers? Only you know. Not everyone, or every situation, is the same. But I'll show you some places to start looking.

Doing a keynote presentation for a company in Oklahoma City, I asked their national sales manager why his salespeople were so successful.

"I take away their excuses. If they say 'people aren't buying', I tell them our competitors are selling. Not good enough. What's your next excuse?

"They may come back with 'our prices are too high'. I tell them our competitors' prices are the same. Not good enough. What's your next excuse?

"'We don't have a good variety of products' they say. I tell them we have more products than our competitors. Not good enough. What's your next excuse?"

The sales manager said that after three or four tries the salespeople give up and go out and sell.

Salespeople are good at finding excuses for not getting in front of customers. They're not good at finding reasons to get in front of them.

The Oklahoma sales manager took away all the excuses so his salespeople could only be left with one conclusion: "The reason I'm not making sales is because of what I'm thinking." He gets them to change their thinking, so they'll change what they're doing.

> *Sometimes our best is not good*
> *enough. But that's no excuse not to*
> *give it.*
> — NCIS-LA

Let me take away some of your excuses. You say you don't know how to get in front of customers. Well, you have cold calling, networking, asking for referrals, social networking, direct mail, email, advertising, trade shows, and marketing to start.

You can't use the excuses that you're too young or too old, you lack experience, you don't have the skills, you need to know more, or you don't know what to say. There are people your age successfully selling what you sell and who know less than you, who have less experience with fewer skills, and who stumble over their own words.

The question my sales manager asked, "Why can't you sell?" made me dig deeper into "why couldn't I get in front of more customers?" What was holding me back? I thought there must be something wrong with me. What was my problem?

I told you that a picture flashed through my mind as I was driving in to work that first week of January. It was the answer I was looking for. It's what coaches want from their players. What military commanders want from their soldiers. What movie directors want from their audiences.

The picture I saw was our December sales meeting. All the salespeople were sitting around the conference table as the sales manager was speaking. Every salesperson had their head down in defeat. That was the answer!

We didn't believe!

We didn't believe in what we were doing. We didn't believe in our product. We didn't believe in the need for our product. We didn't believe in our management.

As I finished driving in, I worked out my beliefs in my mind. First, did I believe there was a need for our product? Of course! They not only saved people time and money, but they made people money. They saved lives because they were used by hospitals, doctors, and emergency aid workers. (Our product was pagers. Our boss, soon-to-be billionaire Craig McCaw, had just started pioneering cell phones the year before and they were still a novelty. Many were even mounted in briefcases so they could be portable. And you paid $1/minute for your calls!)

Did I believe the market was there? Were there enough people to buy enough products for me to make the money I wanted to make? We had four competitors in the area. They had as many salespeople as we did. They were all meeting and exceeding their quotas. The need for our products was constantly growing. New applications were being discovered.

14

The prices were dropping which increased the number of new customers who could buy. So yes, the market was big enough.

Did I believe in the quality our product? Yes. They were made by Motorola, the best communications company in the world.

Did I believe in our management? Yes, because they were constantly asking us, "What can we do to make your job better to make you more successful?"

Did I believe I could sell our product? Yes. But I wanted to take it a step further. I wanted to be a 5% salesperson. A 5% salesperson is willing to do what 95% of the other salespeople *can* do, but are *unwilling* to do.

I found what was missing; why I couldn't get in front of more customers. To be a 5%er, I had to become a *believer*. I had to believe in the job I was doing and I had to believe that I could do what 95% of others could do but were unwilling to do.

Once I got my beliefs in place (it only took minutes), my sales turned that same day. It was like I hit the lotto. My new beliefs gave me the courage, passion, and commitment to get in front of customers. They made it less difficult and more fun for me to do my job of finding the people who had problems our products could solve.

Of course, many factors made our company successful. But our beliefs gave our sales team the courage and commitment we needed to sell. That's the power of beliefs.

What bosses want (and even most of them, like Paul, can't put their finger on it) is a team of believers. Every boss wants their own SEAL Team 6; people who believe, who are committed, and who have the courage to act on their beliefs.

A TV sports announcer made this comment about our Seattle Seahawks before a game they were picked to lose to Chicago. "A team that believes," he said, "is a lot more dangerous than a team with talent." The less talented Seahawks won in overtime.

What makes believing fun is that it's like having super powers. You feel nothing can stop you.

But be aware that one answer doesn't fit all situations. You may believe your company makes the best buggy whips in the country, but you won't have a future selling them (except maybe to the Amish in Pennsylvania). You may believe you're the world's best salesperson, but if you don't have the skills, you're not.

> *All those who believe in Telekinesis*
> *raise my hand.*
> – Steven Wright

Be honest with yourself. Why can't you get the courage to get in front of more customers? Chances are it's what you're thinking that's the problem. Let the question irritate you like it did me. There is an answer. It will probably come from out of the blue. If you keep looking you will find it. I promise.

6

Would You Pull Me Out of a Fire?

You can use this to…
1. Make it less difficult and more fun to start conversations with others by taking the pressure off yourself.
2. Increase your self-confidence and buy yourself time to think on your feet faster.
3. Be the most interesting person your customer has ever talked with.

A young saleslady in San Francisco said that she has trouble talking with older clients because of her age and inexperience. She said she feels awkward and intimidated because she doesn't know what to talk about.

I told her not to worry about her age. I said people my age feel the same way talking with younger people. Like we have nothing in common.

I said, "Look, if I was in an accident and the car was on fire I don't care how old the person is who pulls me out." I told her that you're never too young or too old to help people who want help.

> *The kid has information. Age doesn't*
> *change that.*
> — Rogue CIA agent, *Damages*

As for what to talk about, I told her to take the pressure off herself thinking she has to have answers to everything. Let the other person do the talking.

The rule is that the person who asks the questions controls the conversation and controls what others think about. For example, what color is your hair? What is the name of your high school? What city do you live in? See how easy mind control is?

Ask and you'll know what you don't know and want to know. Asking questions lets others talk about what's important to them, it gives you time to think on your feet, and it makes you a better listener.

The best part? The other person thinks *you* are the most interesting person they have ever talked with.

7

Make Every Day a Saturday Matinee

You can use this to…
1. Master the skills your job requires which will make you sharper and the work less difficult.
2. Motivate yourself to take action by focusing on the process without being concerned about the results.
3. Be comfortable with taking risks and making changes.

Webster's defines "adventure" as an "exciting experience"; "an event involving danger or unknown risks". Think Indiana Jones. Think skydiving. Think about spending the weekend with the in-laws.

What makes an adventure fun is that you get to do what you want to do and you never know what's going to happen.

In the past, what adventures made you want to jump out of bed in the morning to get started? Was it heading out on a long, anticipated vacation? Was it playing sports? Taking up new hobbies? Starting college? You never knew what would happen. But you knew it would be fun.

I'll bet your first day on the job was exciting. It was filled with unknowns. "What's the work like? What's my boss like? What are my co-workers like?" Everything was a new adventure. Maybe now the excitement has been replaced by the routine. What happened? Where did it go? More importantly, can you get it back?

You can. But it's going to require change. Doing things differently. Experimenting with new ideas. Changing how you think. Adventure is about curiosity and learning and creativity.

Adventure is about being uncomfortable. Doing new things you haven't done before. Acquiring new skills. Maybe you want to get into management. Your boss says that you need to improve your communications skills. You need to join Toastmasters.

You join even though you hate getting up before a group to talk. But then you learn that Toastmasters is more than about speaking. It becomes a group adventure in how to acquire better listening skills; how to think faster on your feet. Three important management skills: listening, thinking on your feet, and speaking.

Adventure is not about outcomes. It's about doing. It's letting go and seeing where things lead. Sure, there will be surprises along the way. But isn't that what makes it an adventure? Not always knowing?

Adventure is how you get experience. It's about how you deal with your problems, failures, and mistakes. Randy Pausch, in his *Last Lecture* series said that, "Experience is what you get when you don't get what you want. And experience is often the most valuable thing you have to offer."

This poem by the Chinese philosopher Chuang Tzu has been on my bulletin board for over twenty-five years. Every time I read it I learn something new.

> *When an archer is shooting for noth-*
> *ing, he has all his skills,*
> *If he shoots for a brass buckle, he is al-*
> *ready nervous...*
> *The prize divides him.*
> *He cares.*
> *He thinks more of winning than of*
> *shooting – and the need to win*
> *Drains him of power.*

"You can't think and hit the ball at the same time," Yogi Berra says. Thinking takes the fun out of what you're doing. Pay attention to the job at hand – whether it's cold calling, networking, or working a trade show – without overthinking it and you'll have more fun.

Work is not always about winning the brass buckle. It's more than that. It's about resilience. It's about testing your beliefs. It's about pushing your limits. Your work is about discovering who you really are.

> *We live in a society obsessed with win-*
> *ning and being number one. Don't fol-*
> *low the pack. Rather, focus on the pro-*
> *cess instead of the prize. Even during*
> *the height of UCLA's best seasons, I*
> *never fixated on winning – didn't even*
> *mention it. Rather, I did everything I*
> *could to make sure that all our players*

gave everything they had to give, both in
practice and in games. The score will
take care of itself when you take care of
the effort that precedes the score.
– John Wooden, 11 NCAA titles

Make getting in front of new customers an Indiana Jones adventure. Don't worry about the outcomes. See where it leads. Be curious. Learn new things. Take a risk. It will be fun!

8

Know in Two Minutes What It Took Me Thirty-Five Years to Learn

You can use this to…

1. Turn off your critical, nagging left brain so you can get out of your way and have the courage to do what needs to be done whether it's cold calling, attending a networking function, preparing for a presentation, or asking for the business.
2. Make the difficult task less difficult by making it fun.
3. Think differently, do things differently, act differently.

Fun is what you want when what you want is motivation. So what is – and isn't – fun?

Fun is not the absence of effort, problems, stress, or worry. It's not always doing what you want to do. It's not that things will be easy. Otherwise, athletes will never compete.

No one will start their own business. Parents will never have kids.

Fun is an amazing energy. It excites your curiosity. It increases your ability to learn. It energizes you to act. And – best of all – it keeps you young.

I learned all this from watching that young whippersnapper Coach Pete Carroll lead our Seattle Seahawks to our last two Super Bowls. His players admire and respect him for bringing fun to the game in order to compete to be the best. That's right; he brings fun to the game in order for his players to compete to be the best.

Fun and adventure have no age limits. It could be an infant playing peekaboo with her mom or a 90-year old ex-President skydiving from 10,000 feet.

> *Never play peekaboo with a child on a long plane trip. There's no end to the game. Finally, I grabbed him by the bib and said, "Look, it's always gonna be me!"*
>
> – Rita Rudner

Fun and adventure don't care about your sex, nationality, education, or income. Fun can be spontaneous or planned. It can happen in seconds or over hours, days, weeks, or years.

Fun is essential for work because it gives you passion for what you're doing. The more fun you have, the more you do. The more you do, the quicker you learn. The quicker you learn, the better you get. And you're never discouraged when you're having fun.

The challenge is how to find those occasional moments of fun. One way you can do it is to look at things upside down. Literally.

I've read hundreds of books. If I could take ten to an island, *Drawing on the Right Side of the Brain* by Betty Edwards, an art professor at California State University Long Beach, is on that list.

When her book came out in '79, my dad told me to buy it. I told him I can't draw a straight line and I have no interest in art.

"I know," he said, "but you'll find a way to apply her concepts to business. It will change your life."

It has. It's driven me crazy for thirty-five years. Edwards introduced a concept that led to a question that I have not been able to answer until recently.

To begin her book, Edwards has you make three drawings of people to set your baseline. I drew three stickmen. That's the best I could do.

But then she shows you a most amazing technique. On your fourth drawing she has you draw a Picasso – upside down! Once you draw it and turn it around to look at it, I guarantee you'll be amazed. You won't believe what you're capable of doing.

She stumbled upon this technique by accident. She put a drawing on an easel for her art class to draw while she left the room. On returning, all the students' drawings were on her desk. She couldn't believe what she saw. The pictures were amazing. She couldn't understand what happened in the hour that she was gone. She knew her students didn't suddenly acquire talent.

Retrieving the artwork from the easel, she did a double-take. She found that she had accidentally placed the drawing upside down on the stand. None of the students questioned it. They had no idea what the picture was. So they just drew what they saw.

She took her finding to her friend Roger Sperry who was pioneering his theory of Left Brain/Right Brain thinking. He would be awarded the Nobel Prize in 1981 for his work. She asked him what was going on.

Sperry said she confused the students so much that she turned off their critical, nagging left brain. All they could do was pay attention to what was in front of them. The right brain took over and did what it was told: "Draw what you see."

What Edwards' discovered by her mistake was: (1) it forced the students to pay attention; (2) like meditation, they were forced to be in the moment; and (3) it got them to turn off their critical, nagging left brain to do the job at hand.

So here's the question that drove me crazy: "In work, how can we be in the moment, pay attention to what we're doing, and turn off our critical left brain so we can get out of our way to do what needs to be done?"

The answer – the business equivalent of upside down drawing – is to have FUN!

When you're having fun you're doing things differently. You're thinking differently. And you're acting differently.

And to help find your moments of fun in the tasks that you're required to do, ask yourself this question: "Where's the fun in doing this?"

For example, I was never good at remembering names. Remembering names is hard. Besides, I didn't think it was that important. Then I attended a seminar by Bob Burg years ago. He said that if you want to surprise people and create a lasting impression, learn how to remember names. He said it's weird. People look at you like you're performing some kind of magic trick. They don't know how you do it.

So my question became: "Where's the fun in remembering names?" Here's what I came up with: (1) it's a challenge to see if I can do it; (2) Bob said it's like magic and magic is fun; and (3) it improves my listening and observational skills.

I have to work at it like everyone else. I can't remember a room full of people like some experts. But I do want to remember the people I meet. I still forget sometimes. But it's always fun – even after all these years.

When you're having fun it's like you're in an altered state. What some call "being in the flow"; like when you're exercising, playing golf, or playing a computer game.

In business you may be so involved in solving a problem, negotiating a deal, or making a sale that when you're finished you're exhausted – but elated because it was fun.

When you're immersed in the activity, time becomes distorted. You're not concerned about results. Everything happens without effort. The rewards, the losses, the details – they're no longer important.

And...your critical left brain finally shuts up. You get out of your way and have the courage to do what needs to be done.

When something needs to be done, make it fun and you'll *want* to do it. Make it fun for others, and they'll *want* to do it.

9

Quick, Quirky Icebreakers

You can use this to…
1. Compile a list of icebreakers (singles call them pick-up lines) to decrease the stress of starting conversations with strangers.
2. Listen better to what others are saying.
3. Laugh (laughter releases endorphins in the brain; endorphins fight stress and make you feel better; that and people who laugh are more likable).

For years I've been collecting quirky quotes from television, books, newspapers, reader boards, the internet, kids, yard sale signs – you name it. I avoid the standard motivational "poster" quotes you see bandied about or find in books of quotations. I'm looking for the obscure, unpolished gems that will make me laugh, inspire me or give me hope.

Your assignment: collect your quotes and add to them when you see or hear something that makes you smile or gives you second thoughts. Then come up with your own title for each one to stir your creative juices.

You can use them when networking, cold calling, or working trade shows. Work them into your presentations, to begin speeches, or to post on your social networks. Not only are they good conversation starters, but as the years go by you'll often refer back to them to give you a laugh or to pull you up from out of the dumps.

Following are some of my quotes I've collected through the years. (Over 600 are included in my book *The Wickedly Fun Dictionary of Business – Words That Escaped Me Before My Brain Finished Downloading*.) Enjoy.

Mystery Revealed
"My unstable and bitchy personality is part of my mystique." – *Unknown*

If It Looks Like a Duck, Quacks Like a Duck…
"A rabbi, a vicar, and a priest walk into a bar and the bartender says, 'Is this a joke?'" – *Sid on Father Brown mysteries*

The Lord's Prayer
"Please, dear Lord, don't let me fuck this up." – *Alan Shepard, first American in space, seconds before liftoff*

Maybe – Maybe Not
"You can't turn a 'No' into a 'Yes' without a 'Maybe' in-between." – *Frank Underwood, House of Cards*

Funny
"Humor can be marvelously therapeutic. It can deflate without destroying; it can instruct while it entertains; it saves us from our pretensions; and it provides an outlet for feelings

that expressed another way would be corrosive." – *George Valliant*

How to Eliminate the Competition
"You don't want to be the best at doing it. You want to be the only one doing it." – *Jerry Garcia*

Teaching Is Learning Twice
"If you can't explain it, you don't know it." – *Eric Barker*

Blues Brother
"A lot of people can do what I do. A lot can do it better. They're just not me." – *B.B. King*

Confidence Up the Yin-Yang
"You're often wrong but seldom in doubt." – *Michael Lewis (Liar's Poker) to Stephen Colbert*

You Can't Go Home Again
"The nineteen-year-old marine who sails for war is gone forever, even if he returns." – *Eric Greitens*

The Only Question Is "When?"
"The most wondrous thing in the entire universe is that all around us people are dying and we don't believe it will happen to us." – *King Mahabharata in ancient Indian epic*

Why Millennials are Bored
"It would be boring if you knew everything at the age of thirty-something." –*Jo Nesbo*

Hoofin' It
"(Kentucky Derby and Preakness winner) California Chrome has shown all athletes that you can have a lot of success without tweeting about it." – *Mark Whicker*

And So Is Talking with Your Teen
"Poker is a game of incomplete information." – *Ari Nissim*

Why You Blew Milk Out Your Nose
"Humor is what happens when we're told the truth quicker and more directly than we're used to." – *George Saunders*

What's That Giant Sucking Noise?
"Let the silence suck out the truth." – *C.I.A.*

Possibly
"It is not impossible if it's possible." – *The Hour*

Glad You Asked
"HR director: 'What is your greatest weakness?' Applicant: 'Honesty.' HR director: 'I don't think honesty is a weakness.' Applicant: 'I don't give a shit what you think.'" – *Unknown*

No Different Than Parental Advice
"I meet with my coaches out on the court and they tell me what they think I should do. I ignore them, go back to the bench and tell the players what I think they should do. They ignore me and go and do whatever they want to do." – *Coach Doc Rivers, Los Angeles Clippers*

;)
"My dog winks at me. I wink back just in case it's some kind of code." – *Unknown*

So Is Cold Calling
"95% of all police work is searching in the wrong place. You have to learn to love the other 95%. Otherwise you'll go mad." – *Jo Nesbo*

Let Go of Me!
"Don't argue with an idiot. He will drag you down to his level and beat you with experience." – *Unknown*

Play It Again Sam
"Don't tell my mother I work in an advertising agency – she thinks I play piano in a whorehouse." – *Jacques Seguela*

That Was Easy
"How can I say 'No' to you – and yet I have." – *Nora Ephron*

Honestly
"There's nothing that can discourage people as much as honesty." – *Henning Mankell*

It Doesn't Grow on Trees
"Wisdom comes at a price. And I have paid dearly for mine." – *Sue Grafton*

Gimme Some Hope
"I'm not asking for easy. I'm asking for possible." – *Brad Meltzer*

Don't Quote Me
"Nobody likes being given their own advice." – *The Middle*

Get On in Here, You
"Crawl-ins welcome!" – *Sign outside chiropractor's office*

Flamin' Hot!
"My last girlfriend was pretty wild in bed. She used to cover me from head to toe with oil, and then set me on fire." – *David Corrado*

Then Again...
"Dear Students: I know when you're texting in class. Seriously, no one just looks down at their crotch and smiles. Sincerely, Your Teacher." – *Posted on teacher's bulletin board*

10

It Turned Out to Be a Butt-Dial from a Smart Ass

You can use this to…
1. Practice and master the skill of improvising; get out of your comfort zone; improve self-confidence; prove to yourself that courage comes the instant you need it.
2. Be comfortable in talking with others when cold calling, networking, making presentations, dealing with objections.
3. Improve listening skills; develop sense of humor.

Have you ever left an important interview or an appointment or walked away from an argument and then said to yourself, "Oh, man! What I should have said is…!" Don't you wish you could think faster on your feet?

The *second*-best thinkers on their feet are pedestrians in the crosswalk. The absolute best are your kids when you catch them doing something they shouldn't be doing.

To sharpen your response skills, try playing these games.

Game #1: The punch line game

This is a good way to warm up to your weekly departmental meetings. Have everyone deliver a punch line without the joke. For example:

> "And like my keys, I wasn't lost – I just didn't know where I was."
> "Like the Supreme Court, it's something men will never admit to."
> "And that's how the boss motivates the smart-ass, dumbass, badass, wiseass, and kiss-ass."
> "No discoveries have been made without it. That and it kills cats."
> "Hey! Wanna see my lug nuts?"

Game #2: Fabulous Mystic game

The objective is to lighten up and be able to respond to any situation instead of always trying to be in control. This is a rip-off of an old Johnny Carson skit "Carnac the Magnificent". Put this sign on your desk and have some fun with it.

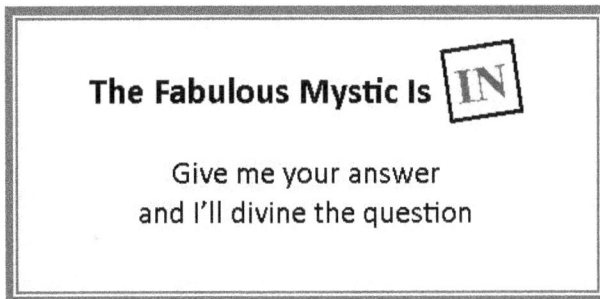

> ### The Fabulous Mystic Is IN
>
> Give me your answer
> and I'll divine the question

For example:

> **yoga** – what does it take to get from the airplane 's window seat to the aisle to hit the lavatory?
>
> **kiss off** – what is the subject line on your email from your last job interview?
>
> **I'm sorry** – what is the best pick-up line men can use because women seldom hear it?

Game #3: Twisted press conference

Once a week call a "press conference" in your company's lunchroom or conference room. Pick out any of today's hot topics in the news. Write the topics on separate pieces of paper and drop them into a hat. One person volunteers to draw a topic out of the hat and be the spokesperson on that topic. The rest of the people in the room will be news reporters asking questions.

The twist is the spokesperson cannot give a logical, well-thought out response. (Kind of like any politician when they're in front of the cameras.) Each answer has to have a touch of humor.

> You're Hillary Clinton speaking on your use of having your own private email server as Secretary of State. One reporter asks, "What were you thinking?" Clinton's response: "Go to hell."

> You're Seattle Seahawk's Coach Pete Carroll being asked by an ESPN reporter, "Why did you call that pass play on the one yard line when you could have given the ball to Marshawn Lynch and won the Su-

per Bowl?" Carroll's response: "He was just in there so he wouldn't get fined."

You're a passenger asking the TSA agent what their code "hot stuff" means. The agent's response: "It's a celebrity who thinks we should recognize him and give him special treatment. We know who he is but we pretend we don't. Then we pull him out of line and give him the third degree."

Game #4: Candid mottos

This can be done individually or as a group. For groups: have someone throw out the name of a company and let people pitch back what their honest slogan should be. Individually: write down the names of three companies and come up with an honest slogan that describes their service or product to you. For example:

> **Sear's**: "The mall's shortcut to Nordstrom's."
> **Wikipedia**: "Pretty accurate…sometimes."
> **NFL**: "Young and stupid should be one word."
> **Google**: "Who needs parents when you can ask us?"
> **McDonald's**: "America's new rest areas with warm toilet seats."
> **MetLife**: "We're betting you'll live. You're betting you'll die. Either way, we win."
> **EBay**: "It's not what you expected. But it's what you got."
> **IKEA**: "Easy to get in. Impossible to get out."

Game #5: Famous last words

Like Game #4 this can be done individually or as a group. Throw out a famous person, profession, or event and match that person's last words before meeting their demise. For example:

> What did the bungee jumper tell the jumpmaster before his last plunge? "Go ahead and lengthen the cord by another six feet."

> What was on Bill the lion hunter's tombstone after his shot missed the charging beast? "My guide was faster than me."

> And this one from Judy Carter: What were the husband's last words to his wife? "The jeans are fine. It's your butt that makes you look fat."

Getting out of your comfort zone and being able to think on your feet gives you the confidence that you can handle anything that happens. So have some fun with it. Practice by playing games that require you to improvise and be spontaneous.

11

The Voice of God

You can use this to…

1. Lower the stress of making a difficult call so you'll project a calm, strong, confident voice.
2. Use your body language to show poise in the face of danger and appear fearless even though you're afraid.

An Atlanta saleswoman told me that when she has to make calls that make her nervous her voice cracks and goes up higher about two octaves, making her sound like she's a cartoon character. She wanted to know what she could do to control her nervousness. Was there any way to lower her voice?

This statement is not fair, but true: people who have a deeper voice are perceived as having more authority. Not fair – but true.

For example, the Allstate Insurance spokesman is actor Dennis Haysbert who played the first president on *24*. Strong, powerful, deep voice. If God has a voice, that's the voice I want to hear.

Now imagine if Dennis Haysbert had the very shrill, glass-shattering voice of Broadway star and actress Kristin Chenoweth. That's why he got the commercial contract and not her.

You may not have Chenoweth's cartoonish voice, but when you make a call that makes you nervous your voice will sometimes jump, giving you a higher pitch. You'll sound less confident. If this is a call to a customer you've never met, you might wrongly get dismissed and never be given a chance for the appointment. Call it vocal prejudice.

The solution? Before making the call, stand and shift all of your weight to one foot. Try to press your foot through the floor as hard as you can. (Make sure you keep both feet on the ground when you do this! Just put all of your weight on one foot.) Standing changes your energy level and attitude immediately. This drops your voice about one full octave without straining your vocal chords and makes it sound richer and fuller.

To prove this, when driving home tonight count to ten in your normal voice: 1-2-3-4-5-6-7-8-9-10.

Then press your foot through the floorboard as hard as you can and count to ten again. But...which foot? That's right. Your left foot! Compare the difference. You'll notice that your voice sounds deeper, richer, and fuller.

Also, you can use your body language to create self-confidence in scary situations by using the "peacock" stance.

Put your hands on your hips, thumbs to the back. Raise your chin slightly. Spread your feet shoulder width apart.

Like a peacock spreading its feathers when confronted by a predator so that it appears to be larger and more frightening than it is, the peacock stance allows you to take up more space around you and warns others to tread carefully. Your body is saying, "Go ahead! I dare you! Give it your best shot!" You won't be intimidated.

And you don't have to actually be in the same room with the other person to use this technique. Before making a scary phone call, take this position for a few seconds and you'll achieve the same level of confidence.

One final thing you can do to calm your nerves is to stand and use the palm-in-palm gesture. Before making the call stand up and put your hands behind you back (palm-in-palm), keep your chin up, and hold this position for about fifteen seconds. You'll feel like you're English royalty looking down on your subjects; it gives you a feeling of superiority and confidence.

12

WAG 1

*WAG is a CIA acronym for "Wild Ass Guess"

1. This has absolutely no value to giving you courage and getting in front of customers, but it will give your brain a break from all the heavy lifting.
2. Objective: See if you can guess the word or words by finding the missing characters from the clue given for it. If you don't know give it your best WAG. Answers at the end of chapter.

__ __ __ f __ __ __ i __ __

#1 Clue: What we seek, never expecting to find.

__ s __ __ __ __ __ f __ __ e __ __ __ __

#2 Clue: Blowing smoke.

f __ __ g __ __   q __ __ __ __ __

#3 Clue: Irritating air quotes to show the speaker is sarcastically quoting someone else without realizing she looks like an idiot. Not to be confused with her one finger exclamations which mean something entirely different.

y __ __ __ __

#4 Clue: The hedge fund manager's bonus paid for with the ROI the investors didn't get. Some are named after candy: "Sucker!" Some are named after secret friends: "The Other Woman". Some are just plain honest: "Stolen".

__ __ v __ __ __

#5 Clue: Gratis criticisms you didn't ask for, certainly won't pay for, and definitely won't take.

__ __ I

#6 Clue: If in the subject line in your boss's email it means, "Get this taken care of now!" In your friend's voicemail it means, "Here's some juicy gossip you'll love." If in your college kid's text message it means, "The doctors think the medicines should clear this up."

___ ___ 1 ___ ___ ___ ___

#7 Clue: When words won't do.

Answers for WAG 1:

#1 – perfection
#2 – sales forecast
#3 – finger quotes
#4 – yacht
#5 – advice
#6 – FYI
#7 – silence

Words and clues taken from my *Wickedly Fun Dictionary of Business – Words That Escaped Me Before My Brain Finished Downloading*.

13

An Ode to Tarzan

You can use this to…
1. Make that first step easier by cutting-to-the-chase with decision makers who think in bulleted points.
2. Set yourself apart from the competition and improve your odds of getting invited back to make your presentation.
3. Think clearly and precisely.
4. Read the comics – and not just for laughs.

When then Secretary of State Henry Kissinger tried to dodge a tough question by saying there wasn't time for a complete answer, reporter Helen Thomas piped up: "Then start at the end."

If you're leaving a voicemail, texting, sending an email, or posting on social media, make your point, make it quick, make it interesting.

The best advice I ever got for how to write came from Roy Williams, the author of *The Wizard of Ads*. He showed me a purpose for something I never cared about in school – poetry.

Williams convinced me that poetry teaches you how to say much with fewer words in more creative ways. For example, this poem on the internet:

> *You and I are friends*
> *You laugh, I laugh*
> *You cry, I cry*
>
> *You scream, I scream*
> *You run, I run*
> *You jump, I jump*
>
> *You jump off a*
> *bridge…I'm gonna*
> *miss you buddy.*

But if you're not into poetry, read the comics and editorial cartoons. They do the same thing. In as little as one to four panels they say it all with very few words in entertaining ways.

For example, in the *Argyle Sweater* Tarzan (who, as you know was raised by the apes) is in the kitchen talking with his Mama Ape as she's standing at the sink washing the dishes in her frilly apron.

Mama Ape says, "Hi, son. I just talked to your sister. She's pregnant!"

Tarzan excitedly replies, "You mean…"

Mama Ape confirms, "That's right, Tarzan. You're gonna be a monkey's uncle."

Or look at the headlines of articles at *TheOnion.com*. They're fun and funny. Take this one: "Fingerprints on Lombardi Trophy to Be Used in Dozens of Criminal Investigations".

One of the best things I learned in Toastmasters is to start with your conclusion first. Most people, when they write or give a presentation, save their best for last. The problem is, by the time you get there you've already lost your audience.

So the next time you send an email, write a letter, or post on your social networks, look at your last sentence or paragraph. That's probably the point you want to make. Move it to the top.

Start at the end.

> *I'm sorry about the long letter. I didn't*
> *have time to write a short one.*
>   – Pascal

14

Please Take the Knife Out of My Hand before I Finish Cutting My Throat

You can use this to…
1. Listen – sometimes the most courageous thing you can do to influence customers; and it's easy because you don't have to know everything.
2. Create a good first impression.
3. Find out what the customer is thinking.

A new college grad complained that she could never land a second interview for a sales position. I asked her why not. "Because they keep expecting me to sell myself, and I can't do it!"

I asked her, "If you can't sell yourself, what makes you think you can sell their product?"

The first thing you sell, the first thing people buy, is your-self. If they don't like you it doesn't matter how good your service or product is, how cheap your price – they'll look somewhere else.

A business owner in Baltimore said she loved the persistence of one of her salesmen. He never gave up. He would never take no for an answer. But she told me he could never close any deals. He rarely got a second appointment. She followed up on some of his sales calls to find out why. The customers said they loved her products, but they couldn't stand the salesman. He was obnoxious, arrogant, and rude.

She asked me what she should do. "Look," I said, "pit bulls are persistent too. But not everyone wants one."

What are some things you can do to sell yourself? The first one takes more courage than you think (but is also *very* easy): ask questions, listen and take notes. Don't think you have to tell the customer everything you know. Find out what the customer wants to know by asking key questions.

As you're listening, take notes. Taking notes forces you to listen and shows the customer that what she has to say is important. It shows that you want to be accurate in understanding her needs. Besides, if there should be a disagreement later as to what was said, the person with the best notes wins.

> *Sometimes you get your best answers*
> *in silence while people talk to feel the*
> *void.*
> – Bob Woodward

Avoid interruptions. The number one complaint customers have about salespeople is that they're always interrupting. If you think the customer is through talking, breathe in for two seconds, hold your breath for two seconds, breathe out for two seconds and then speak. If the customer paused, maybe it's because she lost her train of thought and is trying to get back on track again. Maybe she got interrupted. Maybe she just needed another big gulp of air to finish.

Understand your personality and the customer's personality. Analytical and Driver personalities are turned off by the overly enthusiastic and hyped-up Expressive salespeople. So no, enthusiasm doesn't always sell. On the flip side, if you're an Analytical selling to an Expressive you better step your game up a notch or two.

Be on time. Being on time makes a good first impression. I've worked with salespeople who never even bothered to show up for scheduled appointments. I know because their customers called our office to find out where the salesperson was. When returning to the office, they offered absolutely no excuse.

Customers are annoyed by salespeople who don't respect their time. If you're late it's a red flag. It's like you don't think they're important enough for you to have to plan ahead. If you'll be more than fifteen minutes late, call ahead and ask if the customer would like to reschedule.

Rule of thumb: always be at your appointment fifteen minutes early. It will lower your anxiety level and give you time to "get your act together" before going it. Wait outside in the car and catch up on your emails and texts if you want. But be on time.

At the end of your meeting, and you feel like you have what the customer needs, ask your closing question whether it's asking for another appointment or for the order: "I know we can do the job. But it's up to you. What's our next step?"

It takes courage. You may not like the answer you get. But the only way you'll know what she's thinking is to ask. So suck it up, hold your breath, and let it rip!

15

Can I Call You Ralph? Yes.
But My Name Is Ellen.

You can use this to…

1. Make the first contact easy: let them do something for you; call them by their name; make them smile; let them have the spotlight.
2. Show people they matter; give them hope.

Harvard psychology Professor Dr. Nalini Ambady says that people are "making accurate decisions about whether they like you, trust you, and believe you in *less than two seconds*." And 70% of the customer's purchasing decision is based upon whether they like the salesperson or not.

How do you like talking with someone who never listens? They're always looking over your shoulder to see if there is someplace more interesting they should be. You introduce yourself, they smile, they nod, and then they continue calling you by the wrong name the rest of the night.

Whether you're a salesperson, a job applicant, or an employee pushing for a promotion at corporate, questions going through the decision maker's mind are "How do you make me feel? Do I like you? Can I work with you? How will you make your co-workers and our customers feel?"

No matter how good your skills, no matter how much experience you have or how many degrees are hanging on your wall, if people don't like you then you'll never get invited back for that second interview, if you get invited in at all.

Think of it as having bedside manners. How often have you changed doctors because of the way they made you feel? How many friends have faded into the background because they lost their "likability" factor?

When it comes to getting in front of customers, what are some simple, quick things you can do to increase your likability factor?

This sounds counterintuitive, but it works: psychologists say you have to let *others* do something for *you*. Not the other way around. Get the customer to do you a small favor and they will begin to like you immediately.

If you're meeting someone at their office and they ask, "Would you like a cup of coffee?" always say "Yes" even if you don't like coffee. You don't need to drink it, but accept it as a gift.

Call people by their names. Ever check into a hotel and they call you by your name at the registration desk, when you call down to the front desk, or when you call room service?

Not an accident. Years ago Westin Hotels found that when guests are called by their names they improved the evaluations of their hotels by over 25%. Nothing high-tech. No capital expenditures. Simply calling people by their names.

> *I could never learn to like her – except
> on a raft at sea with no other provi-
> sions in sight.*
>
> – Mark Twain

People like people who can make them laugh. That's where collecting your own quirky quotes comes in handy. You'll always have something new and fresh to share with them to ease into the conversation while sharing a good laugh.

Learn how to talk about things that interest them. One woman consultant teaches classes on sports to women who know nothing about sports. She says that women in the business world today need to be able to understand sports when talking with men because men are not going to be talking about fashions. (I bet she got this idea from the HBO political comedy series *Veep*.)

Don't feel you always have to "one-up" the other person or that you've got a better story than theirs. Let them have the spotlight and keep quiet. If they like you enough to share something personal with you, be gracious and ask a few follow-up questions to allow them to tell you even more. Sure, you may have a better story, but they'll like you more if you listen to theirs. Sometimes listening is the best gift you can give.

When networking and someone asks, "How are you?" the correct answer is always "Good!" They don't really care; they're just being nice and don't know what else to say. No matter whether you're sick, didn't get any sleep last night, or your dog just died, the answer is always "Good!" Besides, if you tell them how miserable you really are they're thinking "Good!"

You don't always have to tell people what you think. People ask me why I'm not crazy about social networking. Simple: (a) I'm a man (let's leave "old" out of it!); and (b) I find I like people more if I don't know what they're always thinking – or sending me pictures of the foods they're eating. I'm okay without knowing.

Give hope. When my wife went to the doctor for help, we left depressed because he gave us no hope. We found another doctor. He gave us hope. And he delivered. She's been fine ever since.

> *Hope is the last thing that dies in man.*
> – Francis de La Rochefoucauld

People want to matter. In small ways you can show them that they do.

16

S&M at Toastmasters Elicits Squeals

You can use this to…
1. Speak with authority and confidence.
2. Instill trust and the perception of competence.

White House Communications Director Jennifer Palmeri was being interviewed by NBC's Kristen Welker about the breakdown of President Obama's Secret Service detail at the White House. This was during Secret Service Director Julia Pierson's congressional hearings when she was asked to explain how a man jumped the White House fence and bulled his way into the East Room. Pierson would lose her job days later.

Palmeri is a very well-spoken, articulate representative of the White House. But on this interview occasion Welker was asking some tough and pointed questions that put her on the spot. Palmeri was clearly uncomfortable.

In the short five minute interview Palmeri's answers were littered with dozens of "oh's", "ah's" and "umm's".

Filler words are killer words; ask anyone who is or has ever been a member of Toastmasters. They have a little S&M game (?) irritation (?) that drives new members crazy. They assign an evaluator to listen to your speech and count the number of "oh's", "ah's", and "umm's" you use during your short three to six minute talks.

Psychologists say that using filler words indicates the lack of preparation. People who use filler words are perceived as less competent. Maybe they're hiding something and buying time to come up with a plausible explanation. They may not be, but that's how they're perceived.

To speak with more authority, know your material. The quicker you can give your information, the more you're perceived as being an expert in your field.

Here's an easy exercise for you. Using your smartphone app record three telephone conversations you have with clients, co-workers, or family. Count the number of filler words you used. Was one conversation absent of any filler words? Why? Was another conversation full of the words? Why?

From now on, concentrate on eliminating your filler words, even in casual conversations with friends and family. Silence has more power than a single oh, ah, or umm.

> *It does not require many words to*
> *speak the truth.*
> – Chief Joseph, Nez Pierce

17

Don't Go to a Party Dressed Like a Piñata

You can use this to...
1. Dress to change your attitude to give yourself confidence that you'll be perceived as an equal and improve the perception others have of you.
2. Make a favorable first impression and get invited back for that next interview.

What's the proper dress for business? Unless you're the Duck Commander on *Duck Dynasty*, when HR says business casual that doesn't mean to come to work like you're on your way to sit in a duck blind at four in the morning.

But if you're a flagger on a construction site, you're not wearing a suit and tie. If you're a pilot for a commercial airlines, you're not wearing cut-offs and a tank top. If you're an undercover cop you dress for the types of criminals you're after.

We all dress up to be who we need to be.
— Douglas, cross-dressing singer, *In Plain Sight*

Look at yourself through your boss's or customers' eyes when you dress for work in the morning. Do you look like someone you'd expect to see working in that position?

For example, how do you expect your doctor to be dressed when you go in for an appointment? If she steps into the exam room wearing a hazmat suit, what are you going to think? If he bursts into the room wearing only his Speedos, how quickly can you be out the door?

Your clothes are your "packaging". You just need to look at Lady Gaga to understand that. Your clothes say "I am powerful." "I am smart." "I am clueless." How you dress affects how others react to you. Wear an orange jumpsuit to the mall with D.O.C. stenciled on the back and see the reactions you get.

Showing up to work in stained, wrinkled clothing shows a lack of judgment. The perception is that lack of judgment would translate to work decisions.
— Jackie Haggerty, HR director

An important thing about the clothes you wear is how they change *your* attitude. When a football player suits up for game day, he's not the same person who visits the Children's Hospital on his day off. An awkward school girl becomes a graceful swan when she ties on her ballerina slippers. The small town's introverted hardware clerk becomes a killer when he dons his flak jacket and weapons in a war zone.

When you go to make a major presentation or go for a job interview, don't you wear your dark suit that means business? When you go to the company outing, aren't you just as casual as the rest? When you want to stand out from the crowd, don't you wear that red suit, bright tie, or classy glasses?

Your clothes send a message. Your choices change your attitude. Dress appropriately.

18

Moms Train CIA Interrogators

You can use this to…
1. Remove the stress from the first contact with customers.
2. Master the skill of asking qualifying questions to get more and better appointments and close more deals.

The *sequence* of asking questions to qualify prospects before going in for an appointment is one of the most critical skills you can learn. The sequence – the timing – is everything. Once you get someone to commit to the first question, they'll be consistent with all their answers to your follow-up questions.

For example, before taking the stand witnesses are asked if they will "tell the truth, the whole truth and nothing but the truth?" An easy, no-brainer question. Once they've said "yes" they're on record to be truthful. Their answers (unless they're habitual liars, con-artists or criminals) will be consistent with telling the truth for every question asked.

The attorney then follows up with quick, easy questions the witness can answer without thinking.

"Would you state your name for the record?"

"And you live here in Denver?"

"Are you employed by Airport Fast Freight?"

Now the questions become a little more difficult. "Do you know the defendant?"

"Would you say you're good friends?"

The questions become harder. "What were you two doing on the night in question?"

"Would you say you'd do anything to protect your friend's reputation?" And so it goes.

You've just witnessed a thousand year old Chinese technique described by Robert Cialdini in his book *Influence: the Psychology of Persuasion* as commitment and consistency.

"A journey of a thousand miles begins with the first step." The journey may be hard. It may be long. Unexpected things will happen. But you have to begin with that first, easy step.

You use commitment and consistency every day and it's used on you every day. You're just not aware of it. Once you become aware of it you can help more people to solve more problems.

The concept is that you ask an easy no-brainer question to get someone to take a stand and go on the record. Then you ask progressively more difficult and more difficult questions until you get to your closing question. Once someone goes on record, rarely will they back down. This technique starts compliance – people want to be consistent with their answers.

Here are three other ways you've seen this technique used:

1. You sell TVs at your local Costco. You notice a customer admiring that gorgeous $7000 Samsung 78" Curved 3D LED TV. You make your approach.

   "How do you like those bright colors?" *Amazing! They really jump out at you.* (That was an easy no-brainer question.)

   "How about that sharp picture?" *It's like I'm there!*

   Isn't that Dolby surround-sound out of this world?" *It's mind-blowing; like sitting in the theater.*

   "Got a room in your house big enough to put that bad boy in?" *I'll knock out a wall!*

   "So…will delivery on Tuesday or Wednesday work best for you?"

2. You do it to yourself. You have a big presentation next week and you're dreading it. You don't know what you're going to say. Finally, you sit down at your computer and at least write down your opening statement. Before you know it, one thing leads to another, and two hours later, the first draft of your presentation is complete. Commitment and consistency. Start small, one step at a time.

3. Even your mom is an expert at it. Remember your high school days? You get home an hour and a half late. Mom's waiting at the door, arms crossed, chin down. "Do you know what time it is young man?" Eh, 12:30? "Know what time you're supposed to be home?" Eh, 11? "Where were you? Who were you with? What were you doing?"

When you harness the power of commitment and consistency, you'll find better qualified customers, make more appointments, and close more deals faster.

Your homework: develop seven qualifying questions you would like to ask every prospect to get an appointment and then number them in sequence, the easiest to the most difficult.

Here is an example if you're a commercial banker and you're on the phone with a local small business. (Note: I can usually disqualify someone within the first one or two questions. If they're disqualified forget the remaining questions, ask them for a referral, thank them, and move on.)

1. I'm sure you do business with another bank in the area? (Easy, no-brainer question. You know the answer too, because you've done your research. But you must ask it as a question to get them to answer and go on record.)
2. Been with them long? (A test of their loyalty.)
3. Is this the only bank you do business with?
4. What kinds of accounts do you have: checking, savings, loans, real estate, investments? (The questions are becoming more difficult.)
5. What do expect from your bank?
6. The next time you're looking for a loan or to make an investment, would you consider looking at a bank who wants to *compete* for your business?
7. Could I make a 15 minute appointment with you, either on the phone or in person, to get a few more details about your business and your goals? (You don't want to do a dog and pony show at this

point. Just get your foot in the door to start building a relationship.)

Commitment and consistency. Make it easy on yourself. Start small. Ask easy first questions. Get increased commitments. Get more appointments. Close more deals.

19

If Dick Cheney Calls

You can use this to…

1. Master the skill of reading people's personalities so you can adapt to their style and be comfortable talking with them in a matter of seconds.
2. Know how much information to give so you won't talk yourself out of an appointment.

Being able to read someone's personality should be illegal. It's like having ESP and being able to predict what they'll do and say.

One way to improve your odds of getting more appointments is to understand personality types so you'll know how to respond to people's quirks. Some people like a lot of information, some want only the bare facts, some want to do all the talking.

Whether you're cold calling, networking, or working a trade show booth, how you relate with the other person will determine if you get that appointment.

There are four basic personalities: Driver, Analytical, Expressive, and Amiable. Listen to the words they use and you'll begin to identify the personality you're talking with.

Analytical	**Driver**
35%	15%
Indirect and unemotional	**Direct and unemotional**
Long words, long sentences	Short words, short sentences
Lots of pauses	They talk; you listen
Skip small talk; stay on point	Skip small talk and details
Give details; be precise	Make quick decisions
Slow to make decisions	Give facts, figures, percentages
Think President Barack Obama	Think Dick Cheney
Amiable	**Expressive**
35%	15%
Indirect and emotional	**Direct and emotional**
The Boy Scouts or Girl Scouts	Like to use "I" and "me"
Calm and unhurried	Favorite subject: themselves
Need small talk to establish trust	Want to do all the talking
Good at reading people	Poor listeners and poor follow-up
Good listeners	Hard to stay on point
Need others to help make decisions	Spontaneous decisions
Think Pope Francis	Think Donald Trump

Drivers are direct and unemotional in dealing with you. They use short words and short sentences. They'll say things like, "What do you want? How long will this take?" Yep. They're short.

Drivers talk; you listen. They don't like small talk. The three words they want to hear from you: "Long story short." They make quick decisions. Because they're blunt, they're seen as being harsh. They may hurt your feelings. They don't care. Get over it. They account for 15% of the people you talk with each day. A typical Driver is former vice president Dick Cheney.

How to talk with a Driver: give them facts, numbers, dollar amounts, and percentages. Skip the details. Speak in bulleted points using nouns and verbs only. Leave out adjectives and adverbs. Don't try to come across as excited and enthusiastic. They're not buying it. Be all business.

Analyticals are indirect and unemotional in dealing with you. They use longer words and longer sentences. They have longer pauses between their thoughts and ideas. They're the slowest of the personalities in making decisions. Think President Barack Obama. They account for 35% of the people you talk with. Drivers and Analyticals make up the majority of Fortune 1000 top executives.

How to talk with an Analytical: you can trade questions back and forth as long as you stay on point. They love details. Be precise with any information you give. They'll check it out. Never hurry them or push them for a decision because they work on their own timetable. If a Driver is a stopwatch, the Analytical is a sundial.

Expressives are the life of the party. They're direct and emotional. They use the words "I" and "me" a lot. Social media has been a godsend and gives them a platform to brag about their awards and accomplishments, to name drop and tell you all the famous people they know, and to send you pictures of the places they've been so you can see how small and insignificant your life must be. They invented selfies. They're great talkers but terrible listeners. They ramble a lot and find it hard to stay on point. Their speech is loud and rapid. They make spontaneous decisions. They account for 15% of the people you talk with. A typical Expressive like Donald Trump has their name on buildings and on private jets so they can remember who they are and where they parked their plane.

How to talk with an Expressive: you can't – forget it. They do all the talking and they're not listening. If you want them to do something for you, don't count on it. Of the four personalities, they're the poorest at follow-up. If there's a lull in the conversation ask, "So...got any pictures of yourself?"

Amiables are indirect and emotional in dealing with you. They're the Boy Scouts and Girl Scouts. They're calm and unhurried when talking with you. They have a lot of patience. They're excellent listeners, ask more than tell, and keep their opinions to themselves. They need to have small talk as they're using it to determine whether they like you and trust you. They go to others to help them make decisions. They're good at reading people. They account for 35% of the people you deal with. Think of someone like Pope Francis.

How to talk with an Amiable: be patient. Start with small talk. Talk about the kids, the holidays, vacations. Be warm and pleasant, slow and relaxed. Develop a relationship to build trust. Don't back them into a corner to make a decision. Try to find out early who they go to for help in making decisions and get them involved quickly if decisions are to be made.

> *An accountant uses his personality as*
> *birth control.*
> – Unknown

Another thing you must know is your own personality type. Don't expect the customer to adapt to your personality. It's your responsibility to meet them on their level.

If you don't know your personality type, ask your friends. They can peg you in a minute. But if you ask four people and one says you're a Driver, another says you're an Amiable, another says you're an Analytical, and the last says you're an Expressive then you are a chameleon. That's a good thing. That means that even as you're talking to all four over your mochas and lattes at Starbucks you're able to match each person's personality. Each person sees you as one of them. The Analytical sees you as an Analytical; the Driver sees you as Driver; the Expressive…well, you get the idea.

If you were to make an "X" in the personality matrix, the personalities opposite each other have the most difficulty in dealing with each other. Amiables have a hard time dealing with Drivers but do fine with Analyticals and Expressives.

Analyticals have a hard time with Expressives, but are okay with Drivers and Amiables. Expressives are taxed by the Analyticals but can get along fine with Amiables and Drivers.

Drivers are in a class by themselves. It's nearly impossible for them to deal with Amiables. They view Amiables as too "touchy-feely". Drivers are okay with Expressives. They love other Drivers because they're of the same breed. Analyticals will drive them up the wall. "How much more information do you damn Analyticals need?!*" Dick Cheney asks Barack Obama.

Know your personalities, and you'll know how to communicate with them better.

20

Would You Like That Egg on Your Face Scrambled, Poached or Fried?

You can use this to…

1. Make the first step easy because you know what to expect and you know what you're looking for.
2. Think on your feet faster.
3. Show why you're different than the competition.
4. Talk with anyone about anything.
5. Know what the next step in the sales process will be.

In the run-up to announcing his 2016 presidential candidacy, former Florida Governor Jeb Bush was asked by a friendly TV host, "Knowing what we know now, would you have made the decision to go into Iraq in 2003?"

It took him four painful, stumbling, bumbling, mumbling days to finally give an answer he thought voters wanted to hear. Every politico, every pundit, every news reporter, and every party leader kept asking the obvious question: "Why didn't he see that question coming?!"

We've all been there. How many times have you walked away from a cold call, left a networking function, or driven away from an interview saying to yourself, "Why did I say that?" Or, "What I should have said is...."

To prepare yourself for every important customer encounter, use the Intuitive Technique to find out what you know, what you don't know, and what you want to know. You'll set yourself apart from the competition because it shows that you've done your homework, the customer will be impressed with your knowledge about his company, and you'll know what to say after you say "Hello!"

Here's how it works if you've landed that appointment, or if you're going to a networking function or trade show to find and talk with a targeted customer:

1. Write down everything you know about that customer. It's easy to find on the internet. Who are the principals? What is the company's philosophy? What is their niche? Why did the founder start the business? How many locations are they in? Who are their competitors? Write down everything you can think of and keep adding to it up until your meeting.

2. Write down everything you *don't* know. What are their intentions? Who are the decision makers? Who are the influencers? How are their decisions made? Why are they looking at you now? Are they bringing in other vendors to compete for this job? Who is their current vendor and what is the problem? What is their budget? Is the company

growing, stable, or declining? What is their credit rating? What if they refer me down to another department? Now you have a starting point for where to start looking for answers. Keep adding to your list up until the meeting.

3. Write down every "Jeb Bush" question you think they'll ask you. (You know they're coming. Don't be surprised.) Why should we do business with you? Why are your prices so high? You all look alike, why are you different than the competition? Who are your customers and will you give us references we can contact? Who handles your servicing when the product breaks, what's the cost, and how fast do you respond? How stable is your business? How long have you been with the company? How do you handle billing? How quickly do you respond to our emails? Can we text you when we have problems? Will we ever see you again after the sale is made? (They won't really say this one, but that's what they're thinking. When is the last time you saw or talked with the salesman who sold you a major product or service?)

4. Write down what you're going to be looking for during the meeting. Learn how to remember names and faces. Memory expert Harry Lorayne says many sales are lost because the salesperson doesn't remember names. (I've included my free ebook *Remembering Names – It's Not Magic If You Know How It's Done* at the back of this book as a bonus.) What does their body language tell you? Are they confident? Are they hiding some-

thing? If they are, what can you do to draw it out? What does their handshake tell you? During your meeting do they allow interruptions from their staff, take phone calls, or look at text messages? What does all this tell you? What is their personality: Driver, Analytical, Expressive, Amiable? Knowing this, how do you deal with it? How much should you talk? Listen? Do they need a lot of information, or just the big picture? How quickly will they make decisions?

5. Write down your next step at the end of the meeting. Do you ask for the business? Ask for another appointment? Do you need to send or gather more information? Ask the customer, "What's our next step? What do you need from me now?" If the customer is non-committal, take the initiative. "I'll give you a call in a couple of weeks to see where we are."

Write everything down. Don't "think about it" or think you'll remember. Psychologists have found that by writing it down you improve your memory and you're more creative in developing new ideas and solutions.

> *When the press talks about my successes as a Senate majority leader they always emphasize my capacity to persuade, to wheel and deal. Hardly anyone ever mentions that I usually had more and better information than my colleagues.*
> — Lyndon B. Johnson

Plus, since it's written down you can slip the information behind some sheets in your legal pad to use as a "cheat sheet" during the meeting if there's a lull.

After the meeting, record all the information you've gathered. Then keep adding to the list until the deal is closed. Every time you meet, every phone call you make, and every email you exchange will bring new information and questions you didn't have before.

When you meet again you'll have answers to give, new questions to ask, and you will be a step closer to making the sale.

It is a lot of work. But if you want to show the customer what makes you different than the competition, it's going to be your preparation, your follow-up, and your ability to solve their problems creatively.

21

What the Hell Just Happened?

You can use this to…
1. Show you're not afraid and make a strong first impression in seconds before you can even open your mouth.
2. Learn how to read the easiest and most common body language clues.
3. Master the skill and art of the handshake so you'll get invited in and not be shown out.

The salesman walked into the CEO's office of a large Houston oil firm to accept the job offer that would pay him a starting salary of six figures. After shaking hands with the CEO, the CEO told him not to bother sitting down. He was withdrawing the job offer immediately.

"You'll have to start looking for a new job," the CEO said. The salesman, stunned, was escorted out by the executive vice president who had to remind him of their earlier conversation just minutes before.

The sales manager with a Silicon Valley firm said that if a job applicant shakes her hand a particular way when interviewing for a position, she rules them out of consideration as soon as they release hands.

The two women, the president and the vice president in a role play with a large southern California newspaper, said that upon meeting a salesman coming into their office for a presentation, they eliminated him before he took his seat.

The Milwaukee salesman said that he could never get a second appointment with the CEO of a company he had called on weeks earlier. To his credit he called her and asked why. "Because of the way you shook my hand," she said.

A professional negotiator in Chicago showed me a handshake he'll use if he wants to intimidate the other party and get the upper hand. A networker at our Denver seminar showed me a handshake he uses to get people to relax and open up immediately. Politicians are famous for a handshake that will make you immediately suspicious. Some people's handshakes tell you that they're uncomfortable with you.

So what's going on?

In the Houston story, while the president and the EVP were in the CEO's office waiting for the new salesman to come in and sign his contract, the CEO said off-the-cuff, "Did you notice how that salesman shakes hands?"

The EVP was surprised that the CEO noticed, but he was aware of the handshake.

The CEO told the EVP, "Tell him that if he ever shakes hands like that again, he'll never work here!"

The EVP got up, went outside, and intercepted the salesman before the meeting was to start. He took him to his office and explained what offended the CEO.

"The CEO just told me that he doesn't like your hand-shake and that if you ever use it again, he'll fire you."

The salesman was bewildered. "What do you mean?" he asked.

"The CEO told me than when you shake hands you turn your **palm down**, forcing him to turn his palm up. He feels your forcing him to be submissive. He doesn't like that. If you do that with our customers you'll make them feel the same way."

The salesman nodded. He wasn't doing it intentionally. He was unaware he was even doing it.

"Got it," he said.

The EVP and salesman went to meet with the CEO. The salesman walked over to greet the CEO. "Guess how he shook hands?" the EVP asked me. "The same way!"

Just like that, the job offer was withdrawn and the sales-man was shown the door.

"You mean to tell me," I asked the EVP, "that he lost the job simply because of his handshake?"

"No," the EVP said. "Now he had two strikes against him. The second was – he didn't listen. I told him exactly what the problem was and what he had to do to correct it. He didn't do it. At this company, with our CEO, at that salary you're not allowed but two strikes before you're out."

The sales manager in Silicon Valley? She said that if a sales applicant gives her the **dead fish** handshake she rules them out immediately. The dead fish is when they just lay their hand in yours as you frantically search for a pulse. She reads it as "you're a wuss, a pushover, spineless."

I told her that's too bad because she's probably missing some good applicants. The dead fish handshake is the most misunderstood handshake in America. And she reads it like most people do, which is a mistake.

I told her to ask some questions about what they do for a living or what kinds of hobbies they have. People who work with their hands for a living, or who have hobbies where they use their hands, have the dead fish hand-shake: doctors, dentists, artists, musicians, even golfers. Their hands are sensitive. The last thing they need is a knuckle-buster handshake that can ruin their livelihood. Also, people may have a physical challenge and they can't give a firm handshake.

The two women at the California newspaper said that when the salesman came into the room, they got up and came from around their desks to greet him. He nodded, said hi, and took his seat. Both women said they would never do business with him, despite his excellent presentation.

"Why not?" I asked.

Without even looking at each other to compare notes, they said, "Because he didn't shake hands with us. We went out of our way to greet him, but he didn't come over and shake our hands. We felt he wasn't treating us as equals. If a man would walk over and shake hands with another man, he better come over and shake hands with us; treat us as equals."

The Milwaukee salesman who couldn't get a second appointment with the woman CEO feel victim to what happened to the Houston salesman.

The Milwaukee CEO told him that, "When you came in and met my three vice presidents (all men), your palm was turned up when you shook their hands. Then when you came over to shake my hand you turned your palm down. I felt you were putting me down. It felt demeaning."

The salesman was embarrassed telling our seminar group this. He added, "I didn't even notice that I shake hands differently with men than I do with women. I've changed. Now I'm always sensitive to how I'm shaking hands with people."

The Denver networker is also sensitive to his handshake. He says he always shakes hands with his **palm up** with both men and women. It relaxes them and they begin to trust him and open up and they don't even know why. It's like you're telling them, "You have the floor. Go ahead. I'm listening."

The Chicago negotiator, if he wants to intimidate the other side, will use the palm down handshake as a tactic (the Houston and Milwaukee salesmen's handshakes). And most Driver personalities will use this handshake just so they can get their message across: "I'm in charge. I give the orders. You obey. No questions asked." That's why I enjoy watching two Drivers trying to greet each other.

Always aware of what he's doing, if the Chicago negotiator gets what he wants he'll use the palm up handshake when departing. He said the other party relaxes and he starts building trust; yet the other person is still not aware of the tactics he's using.

The **politician's** handshake is the most obvious one. It's when the other party cups your right hand in both of his or her hands. They're trying to convey a feeling of sincerity and warmth. "Trust me. Believe me. I'm your best friend."

The problem is, the person on the receiving end is receiving the exact opposite message. They're thinking, "Okay. What are you up to? What do you want? I better watch my wallet!" They don't call it the politician's handshake for nothing.

I had a good friend who was the CEO of one of the world's largest art supply houses. I'd known him for years before he passed away. Every time I went to see him, I'd go into his office and he'd give me the **half-hand**, "Kiss-the-Queen's hand", handshake. That's where they just give you their fingertips to shake.

I knew Bill used this handshake all the time, with me and with everyone we networked with. Knowing this, I'd try to quickly slip my hand in there and give him that **business-to-business** handshake. That's where the outside edges of both party's hands are parallel with the floor and you shake hands going web-to-web at the thumbs.

But I could never beat him. He always beat me with the half-hand. Many people use that handshake. It means they're usually an introvert and uncomfortable in this situation.

When I meet someone like this, the first thing I do when releasing hands is to take a step back away from them. I give them their space. Then I put both hands behind my back – to show them I have no weapons. They will begin to relax; but I make a mental note to myself to keep my distance and don't invade their space.

So what are the lessons?

1. The **best handshake** to use in business is the palm up handshake used by the Denver networker.

2. The **second best handshake** is the business-to-business handshake.

3. The **worst handshake** is the palm down handshake because the other person feels that you're putting them down. (However, if you're negotiating it may be a tactic you want to use to start the bargaining.) If they use the palm down handshake on you don't arm wrestle with them trying to get your hand on top. Simply notice it and let it go. As General George Patton said, "A tactic perceived is no longer a tactic."

4. The **second worst handshake** is the politician's handshake; it makes people immediately suspicious.

5. Be sensitive to other people's handshakes. Handshakes are the easiest body language clues to read. Each tells a different story. Make the necessary adjustments on your part to establish trust.

6. People, like the Silicon Valley sales manager, may read your handshake incorrectly. Work on giving the palm up and business-to-business handshake so people won't eliminate you from consideration.

How important are handshakes in business today? More important than the first words that come out of your mouth.

22

I Wish My Body Would Shut Up When I'm Talking

You can use this to…
1. Practice and master the skills of reading body language to see if what people are thinking is consistent what they are saying.
2. Take the pressure off yourself in stressful situations by putting your attention on others where it should be.

Consider this chapter a tease to get you seriously interested in reading body language. You're not going to master body language in one chapter or one book. Reading body language is a lifetime quest that can turn into a really fun hobby. I just want to make you curious to learn more.

Two books I highly recommend are Joe Navarro's *What Every Body Is Saying*, and Allan and Barbara Pease's *The Definitive Book of Body Language*.

You're already a natural at reading body language. If you're a parent, you can tell if your kids are not feeling well by looking at their eyes. If a teen calls home from college, you can tell by the tone in their voice that something is wrong. When you drop your middle schooler off in the morning, you can tell that you're an embarrassment by the way she scoots down in the seat.

Being able to read body language is like being able to steal people's secrets. Reading body language is important once you get in front of the customer because they may be saying one thing while thinking another. If you can read between the lines to see what they're thinking you can ask better questions and maybe get that second appointment or close the deal.

For example, you know that if you make a statement and the customer suddenly leans away from you, drops his chin, and crosses his arms that he's not buying what you're saying, even though he said, "That's interesting." You know to stop and make a statement like this: "I think you may have a question about what I just said. Before I go any further, can you tell me what's on your mind?"

Not only will he be surprised by your ability to read his mind, but he'll probably lean forward, uncross his arms, expose his palms and tell you exactly what he's thinking.

But what if he covers his mouth or tugs at his ear as you're speaking? What does that mean? What should your response be?

If he covers his mouth, even just for a second, or brushes his lips with his fingers, it means he doesn't like what you're saying. Stop and ask him: "I may have said something you disagree with. Do you have a question?"

If he gives a brief tug on his ear it means he doesn't like what he's hearing. Again, stop what you're doing and ask some follow-up questions. Forget your spiel. He's not listening.

If he rubs the back of his neck his message is clear: you are a pain in the neck. (Note: If he puts his hand on his ass, you've got a bigger problem!)

> *We have an awful lot of members who don't understand that "harass" is one word and not two.*
> – Former Colorado Congresswoman
> Pat Schroeder

What should you do when he rubs his neck? Have him stand up or physically change his position. Or hand him something where he has to reach for it with his offending hand. As body language experts will tell you, the instant you change someone's body language you'll change their attitude.

Proof? Hold your thumb up. Do you feel more positive or more negative? Now turn your thumb down. More positive or negative? How long did it take to change your attitude? The flick of the wrist. Change your body language, change your attitude.

How do you know if the customer isn't being as forthcoming as he can be? If he makes a statement that you think shades the truth, try to recall what he was doing with his lips just before answering. If someone is trying to hide the truth they'll often bite their lip or suck their lips inward just before speaking. Like they're trying to bite their tongue from saying something they shouldn't be saying.

Google the press conference with Boston Patriots quarterback Tom Brady prior to Super Bowl XLIX when he was asked by NBC's Peter Alexander about Deflategate, "Is Tom Brady a cheater?"

A simple yes or no question. Brady smiles, sucks in his lips, then answers. Two things may have happened in those brief two seconds.

First, when he bit his lips he couldn't say what he was really thinking: "Yep. You got me." He was holding back.

Second, since he had to answer, the stall gave him time to find the words to qualify his response so that he would be telling the truth as he saw it: "*I* don't *believe* so." Why not just "Yes" or "No"?

Only he knows for sure, although the NFL had enough evidence to suspend him for four games because they believed he knew. (Full disclosure: I'm a Seattle Seahawks fan and Brady and the Patriots beat us fair and square in the Super Bowl. Ouch! That still hurts!)

Try this one. How can you tell if the customer is confident she has you over the barrel in a negotiation? If she's seated and using the raised steeple position (the hands are in a prayer-like position with the fingers touching and pointed upwards, elbows resting on the table) she's confident she's getting the best of this deal.

If you want to sharpen your ability to read body language, go to a restaurant and pick out one person at another table who is with a group. Watch her facial expressions. What does it mean when she knits her eyebrows? What about when she raises them? Does she lean forward when talking? Lean back when listening? Cross her arms? Do her movements indicate if she's being aggressive or passive? Does she touch anyone? Is she happy? Sad? Angry? Bored? You'll be surprised how much you know by simply observing.

If you're ever in doubt, body language experts say that your actions carry five times the weight of the spoken words.

The second place you can practice reading body language is to watch CBS's *48 Hours*, a real-life documentary of detectives interrogating criminal suspects. This is where Joe Navarro's book is especially valuable since he was an FBI profiler and interrogator.

Watch when an investigator asks a key question like "Were you in the area at the time of the murder?" and see if the suspect leans forward or away from the detective before he answers, how long he takes to answer, where he's looking, and see if he's aggressive or passive in his denial. Good clues to see if someone has something to hide.

Here's a situation you've found yourself in before. You've completed your presentation before your client's group and you're taking questions. You notice the marketing director's chin resting upon her thumb, her index finger pointing upwards next to her cheek, and she has a slight smile.

Three questions: (1) is she having positive or negative thoughts? (2) What does her posture say? (3) What should you do?

Answers: (1) Most people think this is a signal of interest. It's not. When the index finger points up and the chin is supported by the thumb, she's having negative or critical thoughts. She's trying to appear to be interested, but she's had enough and wants this to end. The smile is simply a "courtesy" smile. A real smile will show some whites of the teeth. (2) Leaning away from you and with her arm in front of her torso (like holding a shield for protection) completes the cluster of negative signals that should warn you to do something. (3) The first thing you should do is remember the title of comedian Adam Carolla's book, *Daddy, Stop Talking!* Get her involved immediately. Simply stating, "You seem to have some concerns. Would you mind telling me what you think?" will get her to change her body language and attitude. She'll become actively involved and appreciate that you noticed.

Here's another situation. You're talking with your customer and he's taken the "Figure 4 leg cross" position (used mostly by American men). (1) What is his attitude? (2) Should you challenge any negative comments he might make? (3) Is he ready to make a decision if you ask for the order?

Answers: (1) His attitude is combative and competitive – "bring it on!" (2) If he makes a point, he's ready to argue for that point. Tread carefully. (3) Don't ask for a decision until both feet are flat on the ground. Get him to stand or move so he'll change his attitude.

Let's try one more. You're outside the customer's conference room waiting for all the parties to arrive. You're standing in the doorway, talking with the lady in the chair who's already in the conference room, but you're not sure who she is in the company's hierarchy.

She turns her head as she's speaking with you. (1) What's her likely position in the company? (2) What do her hands tell you? (3) What is her body position telling you?

Answers: (1) Check out the other chairs in the room. If they're straight-backed and armless, she's probably a top executive to command a chair like this with rollers, a swivel, and arms. (2) She's using a raised steeple gesture, indicating she's confident in what she's telling you. (3) Since she could – but hasn't – swiveled her chair to face you directly (with knees and feet facing you), she's not ready for a prolonged conversation with you yet.

Being able to read body language is like having someone on the inside sitting next to you and whispering in your ear what the customer is really thinking and then advising what your next move should be.

23

WAG 2

*WAG is a CIA acronym for "Wild Ass Guess". Give it your best shot if you don't know. No one's keeping score.

$$\underline{\quad}\ \underline{\quad}\ \underline{s}\ ,\ \underline{b}\ \underline{\quad}\ \underline{\quad}$$

#1 Clue: No.

$$\underline{\quad}\ \underline{\quad}\ \underline{x}\ \underline{\quad}\ \underline{\quad}\ \underline{\quad}\ \underline{g}$$

#2 Clue: Wrds wtht vwls.

$$\underline{\quad}\ \underline{é}\ \underline{\quad}\ \underline{\quad}\ \underline{\quad}\ \underline{\quad}$$

#3 Clue: HR spam. A pack of lies prettied up.

__ __ r __ __ __ d __

#4 Clue: To have a better story than the person you need to convince.

__ e __ t __ __ __

#5 Clue: Please God! Not another one!

__ __ r __

#6 Clue: The geek's boss. The richest man in the building.

i __ __ __ g __ __ __ __

#7 Clue: A character witness.

Answers for WAG 2:

#1 – yes, but
#2 – texting
#3 – résumé
#4 – persuade
#5 – meeting
#6 – nerd
#7 - integrity

Words and clues taken from my *Wickedly Fun Dictionary of Business – Words That Escaped Me Before My Brain Finished Downloading*.

Part Two

How to

Find New Business

Using Cold Calling and a Few Less
Invasive Techniques

24

The Holy Grail of Sales and the Wheel of Fire

Finding new business without cold calling has to be the Holy Grail of Sales.

People have been searching for it for since Grunk the caveman called on his fellow T-Rex hunters to see if they'd buy his inventions of the wheel and fire. (He, too, was rejected thousands of times before his inventions rolled to a flaming success through Billy Mays's "but look, there's more" great-great-great-great-great grandfather's infomercials.)

The definition of cold calling has gone through generational revisions. Before the invention of the telephone it was the cowboy knocking on the rancher's door to sell himself as a herder-of-cattle and as the best "gol-durned" bronc buster in the territory. Alexander Graham Bell's invention made it much easier for people in other countries, who you can barely understand, to interrupt your dinners and excite you about their breathless offers. ("Hello, this is…" Click! Mmmm.)

The invention of the television and radio has made it possible for advertisers to… "We interrupt this program to bring you this special offer! Sale ends Monday!!! So come on down!" Yes, advertising meets today's definition of cold calling. But, not wanting to grovel with the lowly ranks of the common beggar salesperson, advertisers are more uppity and call their cold calling "marketing".

The cold calling evolution has now encamped in the computer generation. Google what you want to know for free and don't forget to visit the millions of advertisers (i.e. uppity cold callers) who place their ads on the side to feed the Goohemoth its annual billions in revenues. Facebook, Twitter, you name it; they will give it to you free if you permit them to cold call on you every time you visit their site.

So, by today's standards (not Grunk's outdated *Webster's* definition), what is considered cold calling?

> cold call, v. *Doing anything that is*
> *scary, makes you uncomfortable, or is*
> *risky to initiate contact with strangers,*
> *by any means necessary, to solicit*
> *business.*

Traditional walk-in and telephone cold calls are how most people envision cold calling. But not every service or product can justify such expensive methods of customer contact. You have to look at the profit margin to determine if traditional cold calling is viable for what you sell.

If you sell an expensive service or product, or services or products that can be sold in large quantities and/or that can give repeat business, the traditional forms of cold calling are a must.

Think real estate, cars, communications equipment, building supplies, banking services, investments, medical supplies, computer equipment, manufacturing products, aviation and transportation products, hotel services, clothing or any products sold to department stores and retailers, staffing services – or one toilet seat and one hammer to the government. There are millions of services and products that require traditional cold calling.

And then there are many services and products where the cost-to-profit ratio is too small for traditional walk-in and telephone calls. Look at the thousands of retailers on Etsy. These are individuals who create their own products, work out of their homes, and their profits can't support sales teams or justify making calls to see if someone wants to buy a single piece of jewelry, a scarf, or a handmade purse.

Others who may have to resort to non-traditional methods of cold calling (including but not limited to marketing, advertising, email, referrals, trade shows, direct mail, speaking, and networking) include: authors, artists, musicians, singers, entertainment venues, small casinos, fishing and river rafting guides, landscape services, home repairs, chefs, house cleaning, tree removal services, child care, home care, tutors, street performers, local eateries and millions more. Their services and products have small profits, aren't sold in bulk, and don't generate sufficient, if any, repeat business.

Will the Holy Grail of Sales ever be found? Does it even exist? I don't know. I've been searching for it ever since I got into sales, because I know if I can find it I'll be able to sell it and become the richest man on earth. People have been searching for it since the dawn of man. Until it's found, you've got to be resourceful and creative in finding new ways to let the world know that you've invented the next wheel of fire.

25

If This Is What You Have to Do to Sell, I'm Outta Here!

You can use this to…
1. Get courage by being a coward.
2. Save hundreds of hours and thousands of dollars in interviewing and hiring salespeople.

The branch manager asked me to take a recent college graduate into the field with me to cold call as a part of our interviewing process so she could see one aspect of selling.

Returning to the office, as the grad got out of the car she said, "Tell your manager that if this is what you have to do to find new business, I won't have anything to do with it. I'm no longer interested in selling. Tell your manager I'm not coming back in for the rest of the interview."

By including cold calling as part of our sales interviewing process our company saved countless hours of interviews and thousands of dollars invested in training only to have salespeople quit because they didn't know what it takes to find new business.

I'm still surprised by managers telling me how one of the first questions they get when interviewing sales applicants is, "Do I have to cold call?" Well, yeah.

If people ask me "Do I have to cold call" I tell them not if you can show me how you're going to find new business if this isn't one of your sales tools.

It takes courage to cold call. The paradox is that you can get the courage by being a coward.

Dr. Viktor Frankl was an Austrian, a psychiatrist – and Jewish. At the beginning of World War II he and is entire family were put into the German death camps. Dr. Frankl and his sister would be the only two to survive. At the end of the war he wrote the book *Man's Search for Meaning* where he introduces the word "logotherapy". He's also the father of the phrase "paradoxical intention", which is what logotherapy means.

His concept is that the more you want something, the more elusive it becomes. The harder you try to get something, the further away from you it goes. He said you can use the concept to your advantage, especially when it comes to physical sensations.

For example, you're staring at that 300-pound phone knowing you need to make your cold calls. Your hands shake. Perspiration forms on your brow. Your breathing becomes shorter and faster. Your voice squeaks. You surrender to your fears. You can't do it. You suddenly remember that report that's due next week. You'll make your calls tomorrow.

No you won't. Who are you kidding?

Instead of sweating it, use Dr. Frankl's paradoxical intention to overcome your fears.

Get a Post-It note and write the word COWARD on it. Put it next to your phone or your computer. Try to be a coward when you call people. Try to physically shake. Try to hyperventilate. Try to have your mind go blank. The funny thing is, the harder you try, the calmer you get. Paradoxical intention.

> *Happiness is like a butterfly. When pursued, always just out of reach. If one would sit quietly, it will come and light upon your shoulder.*
> – Robert Louis Stevenson

You've used paradoxical intention all your life, but maybe you're not aware of it. Think back to your high school or college days. You were required to take a certain course in order to graduate. It wasn't your favorite class, but you had to take it. Maybe it was physics or chemistry or English.

Before the final exam you studied until you thought you'd puke. And you still couldn't "get it". Finally, out of desperation, you gave up. Threw your arms into the air.

"There's no way I can pass this exam. I don't understand it. I'm going in tomorrow and I'm going to make the biggest, fattest 'F' this instructor has ever seen. I'll have to repeat this class again next semester."

And you quit studying. Maybe you went to a movie or went out for dinner the night before the big quiz. Everyone deserves a good last meal, right?

The next morning you walk into the exam room, relaxed, confident you'll fail. The exams are handed out. You stare at the questions in disbelief. It seems like they're the only ones you studied all year. You know the answers. You actually know the answers! It's a slam dunk. You ace the test.

What happened? Paradoxical intention. You tried to fail, but the exact opposite occurred.

If you're going to excel in sales do you have to cold call? Yes. Do you have the courage? Be a coward and find out.

(Parts of this chapter were taken from my book and seminars *Cold Calling for Cowards: How to Turn the Fear of Rejection into Opportunities, Sales, and Money*.)

26

Stop Setting Your Hair on Fire

You can use this to…
1. Make cold calling and networking easier to start by thinking of them as lab experiments.
2. Find what others are thinking to eliminate the fear of rejection.

Don Wakamatsu, a former Seattle Mariners manager, was asked what he talks with pitchers about when he goes to the mound before deciding whether to keep them in the game or not.

He said, "You ask questions to see what people are thinking. Not to trick them into giving the answer you want. Only when you know what they're thinking can you help or make changes."

Sales managers say they need their salespeople to cold call but they won't do it. I ask them what excuses the salespeople give. They say, "You name it. It's too hot. It's too cold. It's Monday. It's Tuesday. It's Friday. It's too early. It's too late. It's sunny. It's rainy. It's foggy. The excuses are endless."

Introvert businesspeople know they should do more networking to build up their contacts, but they don't do it. I ask them why not. "I don't have the time," they tell me. Or, "I've tried it before but got nothing out of it."

People would like to apply for another position within their company that's not in their field. But they don't do it because they're afraid they'll be turned down because they're not experienced.

How many times have you wanted to do something but don't because it's too risky or it makes you uncomfortable? How many times have you asked yourself, "Why can't I do it? What is the matter with me?"

We don't take the risk because we're trying to avoid disappointment. We're afraid to fail. It's what I call "pre-event disappointment". You imagine a negative outcome *before* you even act. Out of fear or discomfort you do nothing.

Salespeople who don't cold call imagine rejection. Rejection hurts. It's disappointing.

Businesspeople who avoid networking imagine wasting their time. Why bother? It will only lead to disappointment.

Employees wanting to try another field imagine they'll be rebuffed. Why risk the embarrassment? Why be disappointed?

There's a common denominator: behavior. Behavior is in their control. Results are not. The problem is they're focused on the results. If they want to change their results, they first have to change their behavior.

You get more of the behavior you re-
ward. You don't get what you hope for,
ask for, wish for, or beg for. You get
what you reward.
                            – Michel le Boeuf

When dealing with others, use a sentence like this to change your behavior: "I'll do what I need to do to see what others are thinking, *see what happens*, and respond appropriately."

Think of it as doing a lab experiment. You know the results you're after, but you haven't learned yet what it takes to get them. So you keep trying different things until you hit on the right combination. You'll fail often, you may be disappointed occasionally, but you keep experimenting because that's what it takes.

The first part of the sentence, "I'll do what I need to do to see what others are thinking", we'll come back to.

The second part of the sentence, "see what happens", is about results. These three words take the pressure off of winning the brass buckle we talked about earlier. They remind you that you can't control the results. In baseball, it's like when the ball leaves the pitcher's hand – everyone has to wait and see what happens next.

Business is goal driven as it should be. Goals give you a direction to go. The problem is we too often set the wrong goals. A sales team is given a goal to sell forty widgets a month. A results goal. Something not in their control. It's like a baseball pitcher setting a goal for every pitch to be a strike. Not going to happen. Too much is out of his control.

The correct goal should be behavior goals. For a salesperson it may be to make ten calls a day. Network twice a month. Qualify prospects better. Ask for referrals every time. Master three closes. These are measureable behavioral goals within the salesperson's control. Change their behavior and they'll change their results.

The third part of the sentence, "and respond appropriately", stops you from overreacting. Stops you from setting your hair on fire. What if the pitcher threw a tantrum every time the call didn't go his way? If the umpire called a ball when it was a strike? If an infielder bobbled the ball and didn't get an easy out?

The only proper response for the pitcher is to make another good pitch. Period. If you don't get the results you want, the only proper response is to have a short memory and make another good effort the next time.

But let's go back to the first part of the sentence. "I'll do what I need to do to see what others are thinking." Once you know what they're thinking, you'll know what to do next.

For example, the sentence for salespeople who hate to cold call sounds like this: "I'll make twenty cold calls a day *to see what customers think about their current vendors*, see what happens, and respond appropriately."

The salesperson isn't trying to trick anyone into making an appointment. He's simply trying to discover what people are thinking about their current situation. By asking for their thoughts, instead of pushing for a "yes" or "no" response, there is no chance for rejection.

Ask enough customers and he'll find people who are unhappy with their vendors and who are thinking of changing. He'll find customers who don't use his services and products but are now interested.

The sentence for the networking businesswoman looking to grow her contacts goes like this: "I'll attend the chamber luncheon and *ask every person I meet what they do and what kinds of referrals they're looking for*, see what happens, and respond appropriately." Guaranteed: everyone there will want to meet her because she's interested in them and they're looking for referrals.

And when she calls back to pass on referrals (or even say she hasn't found any yet but will keep looking) they're now going to be interested in her and what she does.

The sentence for the employee who wants to apply for another position sounds like this: "I'll call the supervisor and *ask if I can have an appointment to discuss the job opening* in her department, see what happens, and respond appropriately."

Every business is like a professional sports team. Coaches and GM's are constantly trying to upgrade their teams with the best players available. Players who want to compete. Players who know they can improve.

The employee will either get the job or she'll learn what it takes when another position opens in the future.

If you ever go to Boston, walk their Freedom Trail. It goes for several miles throughout the city, past many of Boston's most famous and historical landmarks. It's quite an adventure. What makes the walk fun are the many discoveries you make along the way.

And that's what makes asking people what they think an adventure: you never know what you'll discover and what's going to happen that will change your life forever.

27

Hey Buddy, Didn't You See the "No Solicitors" Sign on the Door?

You can use this to…
1. Make cold calling easier and have fun doing it.
2. Serve as a marketing tool.

Salespeople hate cold calling. Surprise! Cold calling finds new business, but it keeps a lot of good people out of sales.

A common question salespeople ask is, "Do you go in to a company if they have a No Solicitiors sign on the door?" Of course you do. But it helps if you go in with a gift. This is something that you can run off on your color printer at work.

Hand them the sign on the next page as you make this statement: "I saw your 'No Solicitors' sign on the door, and I wanted to give you this so my competitors will take it more seriously."

SOLICITORS WILL BE SHOT

SURVIVORS
WILL BE SHOT AGAIN!

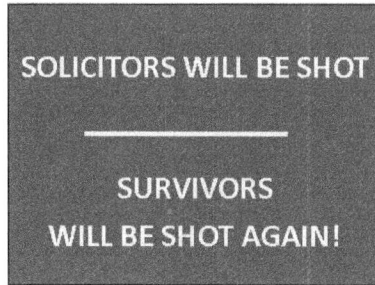

Be sure to print your contact information in a corner of the sign and use it as a marketing tool. I guarantee it's going to be seen, saved, and shown to everyone in the office, including the decision maker who you couldn't get past the gatekeeper to see.

This takes the sting out of cold calling, you'll make others laugh, and you'll open new doors.

That, and you'll scare the hell out of your competitors.

28

How to Throw a Sucker Punch

You can use this to...

1. Make your cold calls easier because you're going to be one step ahead of your customers.
2. Eliminate the most common responses when cold calling.
3. Maintain control of the call.

Doing training with a Chicago bank, the sales managers of their commercial division said a common first response they get on 90% of their cold calls is, "We're not thinking of changing banks." Then their bankers are stumped for what to say next.

"If you know people are saying this all the time," I told them, "then you need to change what you're saying." Why keep torturing yourself?

I told the bankers to lead into their cold calls by taking away that response first, before the customer gets the chance. The customer will never see it coming.

For example, "Hi, this is Marjorie Teller with Chicago Loopdeloop Bank. I'm sure you're not thinking of changing banks at this time, but would you ever talk with a bank that wants to compete for your business?"

What did Marjorie accomplish?

1. She's beaten them to the punch by taking away their knee-jerk response and their ability to steal the initiative. They can't think fast enough to throw out another objection. She gets the time to make her point of the cold call.

2. By asking if they'd ever consider talking with someone who wants to compete for their business, she's set them up for any number of follow-up questions regardless of their yes or no response.

3. She's thrown out a subtle challenge she hopes they'll take her up on: "I'm sure you're not thinking of changing banks at this time." Well...who are you to say I'm not Missy? Marjorie has given them a chance to say, "Maybe. Do you participate in the SBA 504 Loan Program?"

4. She's started a relationship. She's discovering what the customer is thinking. She's made her case. She's made a successful first call.

If what you're doing now is working to get your foot in the door, don't change. If it's not, do something different.

29

I Might as Well Be Talking
to a Statue

You can use this to…
1. Deal with failure and disappointment when cold calling.
2. Make every contact a piece of the puzzle.

Major League Baseball consultant H.A. Dorfman said that Greek philosopher Diogenes was asked by passersby why he begged money from a statute. Diogenes replied, "I am practicing disappointment." Dorfman said that Diogenes was working on his response.

Comedienne Tina Fey says, "The most important thing you learn is how to fail – because most all of what you do is fail."

Movie and TV producer Brian Grazer (*Splash*, *Apollo 13*, *The Da Vinci Code*, *24*, *Friday Night Lights*) says you have to beat the word "No!"

A lady I worked with, our branch manager, commented

that she never saw the value of sports. "It's a waste of time," she said.

I disagreed. I told her that sports is more than a game. Sports is a microcosm of life. You learn how to win. You learn how to lose. And you learn how to deal with disappointment and failure.

Win or lose, you approach the next game with the optimism that you'll do better than the last game. You suit up and come back whether you feel like it or not. You play every game with intensity, even when you know you're no match for the opponent. You learn from every play, every failure, and every mistake. Sports teaches humility and empathy.

Salespeople who cold call fail more than 95% of the time. How do you deal with that much failure, disappointment, and wasted time? Where's the encouragement?

Our best friends and our worst enemies are our thoughts. A thought can do us more good than a doctor or a banker or a faithful friend. It can also do us more harm than a brick.
– Dr. Frank Crane

Do this: think of selling as a puzzle with 100,000 pieces. Even more challenging, imagine you don't know what the completed picture looks like until it's finished. The only thing you have to go by are the 100,000 fragments. Your task is to find how the pieces fit together, one piece at a time.

Every cold call you make is a piece of that puzzle. Every piece is necessary. Everything you do counts even though you can't see how yet.

For example, each call teaches you how to think faster on

your feet. You gain poise under pressure. You become more spontaneous; more confident. You become a better problem solver. You learn how to keep things in perspective. You ask better questions. You listen better. You learn how to read people better. You improve your thinking. You learn persistence. Your people skills sharpen.

Cold calling is basic training for how to become a leader. You can't buy this experience. It can't be given to you. You have to earn it. Experience takes doing and it takes time.

> *Life provides losses and heartbreak for all*
> *of us. But the greatest tragedy is to have the*
> *experience, and miss the meaning.*
> — Unknown

30

Was He Levitating or Was There a Stick Up His Butt?

You can use this to…
1. Keep things in perspective when cold calling and selling so you can deal quickly with the disappointment and move on.
2. Accept that you're not always in control and be okay with that.

Quick, tell me what I'm thinking.

Can't? Disappointed? Why not?

Then why get disappointed when the customer decides to go with the competition? Why get disappointed when you don't get any new leads when cold calling or networking or working trade shows?

Do this exercise and see if it doesn't change your perspective: whether you're cold calling or if you lose the business to your competitor, write down everything you don't know about what happened.

What's going on in the customer's business? Are they having financial difficulties they're hiding? Are they having political infighting? Are they under threat of a hostile takeover? Is the principal under pressure from the board to go with my competitor and I didn't know about it? Was the person I was talking to on their way out of the company and they were taking it out on me?

What was the customer's intention all along? Did she give me a legitimate shot at the business, or was she just looking for a third bidder to give the appearance of fairness? Was I being used for negotiation leverage with my competitors?

What sweetheart deals were offered by the competitor that I was never made aware of? (Think Qatar, Sepp Blatter and FIFA.)

What did the customer think about me, my service, my product, or my company that she never told me? Did someone have a stick up their butt about something or someone at our company? Are they just a bunch of flakes? After being treated like this, would I even want to do business with them?

See? These are questions you have no answers to (except maybe the last one). You can't read people's minds. You're not a fortune teller. None of these answers are in your control. They may have nothing to do with you, your product, or your company. It's not always your fault.

You can't predict the future. You can't control others. (If you have teens you know I'm right.) You've done everything you can do. People get lucky. They have hidden agendas. That's business. That's life.

If you can't predict the future, why be disappointed by things out of your control? You've gained some new experiences. Learn from them and move on.

I know what you're thinking. You're think-
ing I can read your mind.
– Cal FitzSimmons

31

Best Two Out of Three?

You can use this to…
1. Start cold calling even though you're uncomfortable.
2. Stop second guessing your decisions.

Maybe you're new in sales or new with your company. You're indecisive as to whether you have enough training and information to start cold calling your territory.

Really? How much more information do you need? Aren't you just procrastinating? If you believe that your product will do as advertised, that's enough to get started. You'll figure out the rest as you need it.

But if you still can't pull the trigger, learn from football. They flip a coin to get the game started. Heads or tails, their goal is the same: to win. They may not start from where they want, but the game is long – and there are many ways to score.

Flip a coin. Heads, you have enough information. Make your calls. Tails, you don't have enough information. Make your calls anyway.

Decisions are merely starting points. Accept that once the decision is made, adjustments will have to be made. That's okay. That's part of the game. Those who can adjust best win.

Dr. Maxwell Maltz (*Psycho-Cybernetics*) said, "There are few inherently right decisions or wrong decisions. Instead, we make decisions, then make them right."

But this doesn't mean all decisions need be decided by the flip of a coin. For example, if you're in the Super Bowl, you're on the opponents one yard line, you're in a position to make history, you have the best running back in the NFL, you have three downs and one time out in your hip pocket with twenty seconds to go, you don't flip a coin to see if you're going to throw a pass over the middle to the back-up receiver. Some decisions are just no-brainers!

Here's another situation. You've made a decision to take the promotion that's been offered. But now doubt starts creeping in. You can't sleep because you keep second-guessing yourself.

Once the decision is made, don't second-guess yourself. If you do this too many times, you'll be afraid of making any more decisions. Worse, you'll undermine your leadership because people can't trust you to be decisive.

So make your decision. If you think you'll second-guess yourself, take a quarter and throw it as far as you can. Throw it down the street. Throw it into the lake. Throw it into the bushes. That quarter represents your decision. You can never worry about that decision again unless you go back and find that specific quarter and hold it in your hand. Then you can worry all you want.

What you'll discover is that you'll never go back to find that quarter. You'll find the worry over that decision isn't worth two-bits.

By the way, after our Seahawks lost in the last twenty seconds, I went out on our back deck and threw a quarter as far as I could into the woods. I still go out every day trying to find it.

32

Quit Scaring the Bejesus Out of People You Network With

You can use this to…

1. Muster the courage to take the initiative to introduce yourself at networking functions.
2. Increase your referrals.

It's interesting to watch members gather at a chamber of commerce meeting before the program starts. The majority come in by themselves, or in small groups, and find a seat at the most remote table possible and immediately get on their smartphones or tablets instead of meeting and talking with others.

The irony is that chamber meetings are for meeting strangers and, well, networking. But most people keep their heads down for fear of meeting strangers.

*Fear makes strangers of people who
should be friends.*
– Shirley MacLaine

Being a speaker at many chamber meetings, I like to ask the introvert members why they don't mingle. After a little hemming and hawing they fess up: they feel the other members will try to sell them something. They don't like the pressure of having to listen to their spiels or being cajoled into making an appointment. The main reason they attend is because they don't have enough business to begin with; and they don't have a clue for how to find it. Besides, they don't have the money to buy anything anyway. They have told me they thought the purpose of the chamber was so members could sell to members.

I'm surprised that chambers don't show their members how to better connect with each other so they won't scare the bejesus out of each other.

The way I avoid scaring others is to introduce myself and quickly add, "I don't think you'd ever be a prospect for what I sell, and I may not be one for you. But if you tell me what your customers look like I'll see if I can get you some referrals."

This immediately takes the pressure off them feeling I'm going to back them into a dark corner somewhere and hold them hostage until they give up their first born. (Although some have offered.) And it stops them from trying to sell me. With this technique I've made a friend for life because they know I might be able to send new business their way.

What members need to understand is that you don't need to sell to the other members. That's a very small circle of prospects.

What you want is access to the people they know. With social networks and the internet what it is today, *each* person knows hundreds of people you don't know. And that's what you want: for them to mention you or introduce you to the people they know.

33

A STUPID Tattoo on the Forehead Is a Bridge Too Far

You can use this to…
1. Have people initiate conversations with you at networking events and trade shows.
2. Create an "anchor" that gets people to easily remember you.

Checking in at the Ritz-Carlton in St. Louis to do one of our presentations, I asked the front desk clerk why their nametags also had the names of their hometowns on them.

She smiled and said that because many of their staff are introverts, this is like an invitation for guests to initiate a conversation with them. She said someone may see she's from Philadelphia and make a comment about visiting or being from that area and voilà it's like they're friends with common interests.

At some networking events attendees do wear nametags. At most trade shows vendors and attendees wear nametags.

When you get yours, slip the name of your hometown under your name. You'll be surprised how many people will start conversations with you.

A variation is to put your hometown on your business card. After the event people may forget your name or your company name, but they'll likely remember, "Oh, it's that guy from Chugwater, Wyoming," and they'll dig your card out of the pile.

Former Secretary of State Madeleine Albright has over 200 brooches and pins she wears at different times to express her opinions and moods. A business owner in North Carolina said she's taken Albright's idea and wears a different brooch each day. She said people always find something to comment about when seeing one. She said it's like a "reverse cold call" where people will initiate contact with her first.

Men's ties can do the same thing. (Finally, there's a purpose for ties after all?) And isn't that why people wear T-shirts with sometimes outrageous sayings or pictures on them so others will notice them and make comments. Of course, a tattoo on the forehead does the same thing. But that would only be stupid, unless the tattoo actually said "STUPID".

> *I saw a woman wearing a sweatshirt*
> *with "GUESS" on it. I said "thyroid*
> *problem?"*
> – Unknown

I had dinner with a car dealer in Little Rock, Arkansas, named Cadillac Jack over twenty years ago. I remember him not just because of his ability to brand his name, but because of his business card. On the back he had listed the phone numbers of the president of the United States, the Pope, and other heads of state.

Networking is all about meeting new people, having intriguing conversations, and getting them to remember you when they need you or when they can tell their friends about you.

34

When I Said "Follow Me" I Meant on Twitter

You can use this to…

1. Create a buzz with your social networks and emails to increase referrals.
2. Keep in touch on a monthly basis without wearing out your welcome.
3. Separate yourself from the competition.

The easiest contacts to make are through referrals. The trick is coming up with a program to get them. Here is something simple that you can do with your email and social networks to create your own personal marketing pieces.

You don't need a lengthy newsletter or blog. That takes too much time and effort and no one will take the time to read them (thus, the creation of Twitter).

Do this: send or post something that is quick and entertaining. If you remember what postcards used to look like, that's your goal. When people get it, they can't wait to open it and then pass it on to other departments, co-workers, friends, and family. (Yes, they really will!) This is where your referrals will come from.

Make it humorous, fun, or thoughtful. You don't need to include any personal notes on the cards. But do include your contact information. Maybe a quick line or two about what you sell.

If you're using email and have a customer database, there are several internet programs like ConstantContact.com and MailChimp.com that you can use. Or simply post them on your Facebook. Here are some of my cards to give you an idea.

Jerry Hocutt
Author

The Wickedly Fun Dictionary of Business: Words That Escaped Me Before My Brain Finished Downloading

jerry.ht@footinthedoor.com
www.FootInTheDoor.com

Jerry Hocutt
Author

Cold Calling for Cowards: How to Turn the Fear of Rejection into Opportunities, Sales, and Money

jerry.ht@footinthedoor.com
www.FootInTheDoor.com

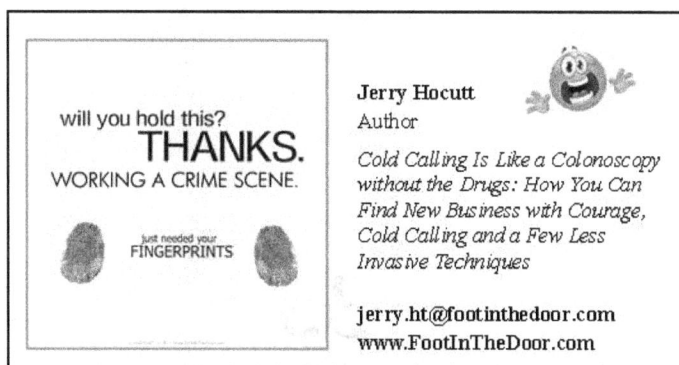

If you need photos or artwork to put on your cards there are several websites with inexpensive ones that you can purchase.

Send the cards to both your prospects and customers. Collect names at trade shows and when cold calling to build your list. Send them to people you network with.

Every person you contact knows hundreds of people you don't. You want access to their friends, and this is how you get it. It's an easy way to keep in touch with your customers and prospects once a month without wearing out your welcome, and you'll both have fun doing it.

Guarantee: This will separate you from your competitors. It will get others to remember you first when they're ready to buy, or when they can refer someone to you who wants to buy what you sell.

35

Bribes Are Not Just for FIFA and Politicians

You can use this to...

1. Get referrals from a company's "Contact Us" page.
2. Get the decision maker's name most every time.
3. Get permission to contact the decision maker by email.

If you want to get in to a company and don't have any contacts there are several ways to do it.

You can do a walk-in cold call or make a telephone cold call. I won't go into details here because I cover the subject extensively in my book *Cold Calling for Cowards*® as well as several other books I have on the subject.

You can network. Excellent way to get your foot in the door. You can get referrals; the best way to get introduced to others. Social networking works.

But what about emailing someone from out of the blue? Isn't emailing like an electronic cold call? It is. But, like calling on a company that has the "No Solicitors" sign on the door, it will work if you do it right. And it's not as scary.

Your objective is to get someone in the company to give you the name of the contact you're looking for and permission to email them. Go to the company's "Contact Us" page on their website. It's there for anyone who wants to contact their company. Consider it an electronic gatekeeper. Send a brief email. And when I say brief, keep it to two or three very quick paragraphs. Offer an inducement (a.k.a. in political circles, a "bribe") to get the name. Below is one of my emails that has been very successful.

> I'm giving away a copy of my ebook *Lunch? – 20 Sales Questions I've Been Asked Over Lunch* to your business development manager to pass on to your sales team. I'm doing this to introduce my new book *The Wickedly Fun Dictionary of Business – Words That Escaped Me Before My Brain Finished Downloading*.
>
> Can you tell me who I can contact to see if I can email them this information?
>
> Thanks!
> Jerry Hocutt
> Author, Speaker and Sales Trainer
> www.FootInTheDoor.com

I've been amazed by how easy it is to get names this way. Every reply has the name and email address I need. The returned email also includes the name of the assistant responding. I now have a referral.

When I contact the business development manager my email looks like this:

Subject: Referred by Jill Haddock

Hi Teresa,

Jill referred you to me and said you might be interested. I'm giving away my ebook *Lunch? – 20 Sales Questions I've Been Asked Over Lunch* that you can pass on to your sales team.

I'm doing this to introduce my new book *The Wickedly Fun Dictionary of Business – Words That Escaped Me Before My Brain Finished Downloading*. The ideas in the book will help to make their work a little more fun.

If you're interested in receiving Lunch and a Wicked flyer, simply return this email and I'll send them today.

Thanks –

Jerry Hocutt

Author, Speaker and Sales Trainer

www.FootInTheDoor.com

Points to consider:

1. Treat your email subject line like the headline on a news story: it's the most important part of your email. It will either get the email opened or deleted. I used "referred by Jill Haddock" in the subject line to Teresa.

2. I didn't send the attachments to Teresa on the first email because I haven't received permission to do so yet. Never send attachments without permission!

3. I have something (hopefully) she wants: answers to sales questions that will help her sales team to be more productive. I immediately state that I'm *giving* the ebook away to let her know there's nothing to buy.

4. Since people know there is always a catch if something is free, I don't hide it. I'm upfront. The catch is I want to send a flyer to introduce my book.

5. I leave the decision to Teresa. If she's interested she can let me know.

6. I make it easy for her to request Lunch by simply returning my email. Nothing else. Sometimes people return the email, no notes. Sometimes they say "Thanks!" Sometimes they give me lengthy notes.

7. I include my website so they can check me out to see that I'm legitimate before they contact me if they want.

8. Beneath my signature I'll include a graphic of the cover of the book since pictures capture people's attention.

Make sure all your emails are quick and to the point. If they open an email and see several wordy paragraphs from someone they don't know they won't read it.

The "gift" should be something they can use that will help them in their business (*not* a product brochure) and something that can be sent via email. Best of all, you want it to be something they want to pass on to others to increase your referrals.*

Do people get upset with the emails? No. If I send 2000 emails over time, maybe one will say "remove from list". No problem. This has proven to be the easiest way to get the decision maker's name and get my message in front of them...ever! On a promotion like this I never contact them more than once unless they reply.

Emails work, if you do them right.

---

*FREE: If you don't have a gift, I have some free ebooks on my site that I can send to you with content that applies to anyone in business. I can even put your name or company name on the cover of the book as "Compliments of (Your Name)". Email me at jerry.ht@footinthedoor.com for information.

36

Come Closer – Let's Scratch Each Other's Back

You can use this to…
1. Get others to promote you to all their customers.
2. Help your contacts to find new customers for their business.
3. Use as free trade show giveaways.

It would be nice if you could get other companies to tell all their customers about you. You can, but you have to help them find new business for their companies too. You can do both with an easy cross-promotion.

I've done this successfully with other companies. It's simple and very inexpensive. (Think of your kids' allowance as being even more expensive.)

If a company or group will send one of my free PDF ebooks to their customers or members, I'll give them an inexpensive one-page ad inside the ebook to promote their chamber, company, or upcoming event. (A PDF ebook can be read on any computer, tablet, or smartphone and forwarded by email to anyone.)

The group gets an inexpensive marketing/advertising piece. When their customers get the ebook they'll pass it on to *their* contacts thus promoting, and in effect endorsing, their company.

Companies can give the ebooks to everyone on their customer list, and give them away when cold calling, networking, when customers call in for information and at trade shows.

Giving them away at trade shows gives their salespeople an excuse to capture visitors' emails. After emailing the download, the salesperson can add, "I know you'll get some ideas you can use from the book. I'll give you a call next week and see what you think." The salespeople now have a reason to follow-up on their trade show leads.

If you want to create your own ebook giveaway make sure it's not an overblown company brochure. You want to have entertaining content; not a twenty-page advertisement. It doesn't have to be long; maybe ten to twenty pages. You could have your staff contribute their favorite quotes. Or photographs. If you have a blog, include some of your articles. Maybe business tips. You want something they'll pass on to those they network with so you'll get referrals while they create goodwill and get referrals for themselves as well.

The next two pages have samples of ads that have been included in some of my ebooks that chambers have sent to all their members.

If you don't have the time to create your own ebooks and would like to use mine for your company or group, email me for the details at jerry.ht@footinthedoor.com.

YOUR Chamber at Work For YOU

THE GREATER
PALM BAY
CHAMBER
OF COMMERCE

- Are you making all the sales you want to make?
- Would you like to learn how you can increase your sales?
- Do you want your sales staff to be more productive?
- Are you interested in learning a new way to increase your profits?

If you answered YES to these questions, then take a few moments to read "LUNCH? - 20 Sales Questions I've Been Asked Over Lunch" by Jerry Hocutt and learn some new and profitable techniques to turn your sales staff into Super Stars.

This pdf E-book is being provided to you at no cost by the Greater Palm Bay Chamber of Commerce as a way of saying "Thank You" for being a member. Feel free to pass it on to business acquaintances that you feel will benefit from reading the book.

Greater Palm Bay Chamber of Commerce

Vicki Northrup / President & CEO

4100 Dixie Highway NE

Palm Bay, FL 32905

321.951.9998 / www.GreaterPalmBayChamber.com

E-mail: info@greaterpalmbaychamber.com

TASTE of Tumwater
& BIZ EXPO

Presented by Tumwater Area Chamber of Commerce
November 3, 2012

Food and wine/beer pairings; jazz; chef cooking demos; trade show and high-end artisans – something for everyone! Join us for this fun, savory event. Help us "Name the Chef". There will be three awards given for:

- Golden Fork Award– best "Taste of Food"
- Best Booth Award – most interactive fun booth
- Gold Medal Award-best "Taste of the Day " for a winery or brewery

Showcase your business as a sponsor or booth registrant. Tickets go on sale early October.

For additional information visit www.tumwaterchamber.com
or call 360.357.5153.

Tumwater Area
CHAMBER OF COMMERCE

Promote, support and advocate for area businesses.

Morning Power Hour Networking Breakfast – 2nd Tuesday of each month.
Monthly Lunch Forum – 3rd Tuesday of each month.
Call 360.357.5153

37

WAG 3

*WAG is a CIA acronym for "Wild Ass Guess". Give it your best shot if you don't know. No one's keeping score.

___ ___ h ___ c ___

#1 Clue: Not even a speed bump between lobbyists and politicians.

___ o ___ f ___ ___ ___ ___ ___

#2 Clue: Watch this!

___ ___ ___ ___ ___ ___ z ___

#3 Clue: What women look for men to do. That's not happening.

___ ___ e ___

#4 Clue: A thought that seemed good at the time. Why second thoughts are better.

___ ___ k ___ ___

#5 Clue: Corny. Not an Arkansas mispronunciation for hockey.

___ k ___ ___ ___

#6 Clue: What you acquire from correcting your mistakes.

___ ___ y ___ r ___

#7 Clue: Like those in the witness protection program, they're the hardest people in the world for salespeople to find even though they're walking around in plain sight.

Answers for WAG 3:

#1 – ethics
#2 – confidence
#3 – apologize
#4 – idea
#5 – hokey
#6 – skill
#7 – buyers

Words and clues taken from my *Wickedly Fun Dictionary of Business – Words That Escaped Me Before My Brain Finished Downloading.*

38

Trade Show Hymns

You can use this to…
1. Meet "hot-to-buy" customers the easiest way possible – they're coming to you.
2. Stand out from 86% of your trade show competitors.
3. Break down barriers between you and your visitors.

Mustering for roll call when in tech school at Keesler AFB in Biloxi, Mississippi, we would sometimes sing hymns while standing at attention at 7 a.m. The hymns were sung for particular people who got on our squadron's bad side by doing stupid things that affected our jobs. They were pretty simple and went like this:

> *Hiiiim*
> *Hiiiim*
> *F**k him*

One day our squadron commander happened to be passing by and heard our little sing-a-long. We were ordered to stop doing such childish things or face reprimands.

We sang a hymn for our commander the next morning.

I think anyone who's ever worked a trade show would occasionally like to sing a hymn to honor the event, especially when the trade show is bombing or things are dragging.

> *Groan*
> *Moan*
> *Gimme back my smartphone*

Or maybe you'd just like to repeat Larry Verne's ditty from the famed 7th Cavalry's march to the Little Bighorn:

> *Please, Mr. Custer*
> *I don't wanna go!*
>
> *(Forward, Ho!)*

It's rare to see salespeople jumping for joy to work trade show booths. (Owners are different. Since it's their money invested, they're always up for it.) When time assignments are doled out, most salespeople are looking for excuses not to man up.

What salespeople fail to realize is that working the booth is accomplishing exactly what they want – to get in front of the people who can buy.

According to the Trade Show News Network, 81% of trade show attendees have buying authority. They're the decision makers salespeople look for. And 67% of all attendees represent a new prospect. The number one reason attendees come is to see new products.

Walk around the exhibition area when you're not working your booth and you'll confirm these findings: only 8% of the salespeople working the booth will walk over and initiate contact with prospects standing on the perimeter of their booth looking in. Yet 76% of these prospects will be more open and talkative with the salesperson who says "Hi" and are twice as likely to remember them by name.

Watch the salespeople working their booths. Many will stay at the back of the booths, engaged on their smartphones or talking with co-workers. They're afraid to engage. A simple nod of recognition that the prospect is alive and standing there is a good start.

Look at the attendee's nametag. If you can see what city they're from, use that as an icebreaker. "I see you're from St. Louis. I went up in the Arch once. Man, those little cars that take you to the top are not good news for the claustrophobic."

If they step forward and make friendly sounds, it's okay to be curious. Ask them what they've seen so far. What the strangest thing is they've seen. The most surprising thing. How many trade shows do they attend each year? Ask them what they're looking for at the show.

Most booths have a fishbowl or something similar for visitors to drop in their business cards for a drawing so companies can get names to follow up on. Yet 86% of the people who leave their cards are never called back. And most are decision makers looking to find solutions to their problems. They have needs, wants, and money. They're looking to make changes and are ready to make decisions. Not following up on trade show contacts is one of management's biggest complaints, especially for the monies they've invested.

Sure, they may have stopped by to enter the drawing. And when you call back to follow up they may tell you as much. That's okay. Ask them if they know anyone they network with who might be interested in what you sell. If nothing else, use the follow-up to practice your sales skills.

You don't need to be smarter than your competitors. You just need to follow-up because 86% of them don't.

One final thing. Too many booths have a table or desk at the front of their area to establish their border. Get rid of it. Trade show managers say that vendors who have open booths get more foot traffic inside the booth and it leads to better conversations and relationships. Subconsciously, visitors see the table as a closed door warning them to "Keep Out!"

Don't treat your trade show as a nuisance. It's attracting the types of buyers you're looking for. It's your responsibility to take the initiative and make things happen.

You can start with "Hi."

39

Be the Master of Your (Small Business) Domain

You can use this to…
1. Cross-sell and get add-on business with current customers.
2. Turn prospects into customers.
3. Create a bigger, better customer database.
4. Get permission to keep in touch on a monthly basis and increase customer retention.
5. Have your own mini-trade shows without the expense and without leaving home.
6. Increase referrals.

The majority of small businesses can't afford the commitments of time and money to participate in trade shows. But that's not to say they can't do their own shows – and have better results than the professionals.

Leads are walking in to your office every day. But because they're so familiar you can't see them. Current customers. They're standing in your reception area now. They're leaning on your counter talking to your service people. They're calling and talking with your salespeople and customer service reps.

These are people who can give you add-on business today, new sales tomorrow, and referrals every day. They're more qualified than any traditional trade shows can attract. But they're people you let walk out the door without getting permission to market to later.

Is it because you don't know what to say? Or how to capture their information? Or what to do with it once you get it? Or (hopefully not!) just too lazy?

Chances are your company has two points of contact with customers every time they walk through your doors: your front counter (or reception area) and your service counter. Areas that you can establish as your own mini-trade show domains. Areas where you can cross-sell, get referrals, and prime customers for future sales.

After taking care of their needs, why don't you get their emails for marketing? Like at trade shows, have drawings for prizes. Put a fishbowl on your front counter and service counter. Tell them there is only one requirement: only those with emails are eligible because that's the only way you'll be contacting them.

Let people know that once they've entered for one drawing, they'll be entered for all the monthly drawings. All you want to do is build your customer database. Their one time entry is all you need. Then have one drawing each month.

The drawings serve two purposes. First, it gets important email addresses. Second, you get permission to email and market to them each month. In effect, you establish a monthly keep-in-touch program. (See a simple marketing email at the end of this chapter. It took me ten minutes to create this from scratch.)

A monthly giveaway gives you a reason to stay in touch, because chances are that no one from your company has called on them for months.

But what if you're in outside sales and your company doesn't get much walk-in business, or your customers are spread across the country? Will this still work? Of course.

When people contact you by phone or on the internet about your services and products let them know about your monthly drawings. Tell them all customers *and prospects* are eligible to win. Tell them all you need is their name and email address to be eligible and they'll be entered for the prizes.

If you're cold calling or networking, start your own trade show-on-wheels and collect prospects' business cards and info. Even if they're "not interested" in what you sell, get their names and emails for the drawings.

By allowing prospects to enter the drawings without be-coming customers, you're building relationships with them that will eventually pay off. You'll be having more contact with them than they have with their own vendors. It's what I call positioning yourself to be the #2 vendor on their list. If you can't be their #1 vendor, you better make sure that you're #2, because when things change – and they will – they're not calling #3, #4, or #5. They're only calling #2.

Your monthly emails may be just the reminder they need to place the new order they've been putting off. You'll be the first person they think about when talking with their friends who may need what you sell. Use the emails to introduce new services and products. Ask for referrals or introductions to new departments or branches.

Your monthly contacts will keep your competitors at bay. After all, your customers are seeing and talking with your competitors five times more often than they're talking with you. Let your customers and prospects know that you're still here and that they're important and not forgotten.

Create your own mini-trade shows. No travel. No expenses. Better leads. Reasons to connect. You'll be the master of your small business domain.

Our Small Business, Inc.

Congratulates

Ben Snicker of Snicker, Snicker & Snort P.S.

This month's winner for dinner for two at the beautiful Salish Lodge.

Did You Know?

1. The mansion on top of the hill at Arlington National Cemetery belonged to Robert E. Lee at the beginning of the Civil War.

2. When Lee left the mansion, the Union buried its first troops in his wife's garden to make sure they'd never want to return.

3. At the base of the hill is the grave and eternal flame for John F. Kennedy.

Use this area for trivia to get and keep their attention. Can have employees contribute with their ideas, photos, etc.

Use an area like this to introduce new services or products.

Tell about next month's drawing and remind them they're automatically entered since they've already signed up.

Give a plug to the winner of this month's drawing and their business.

Introduce new employees.

Andy Jackson Referral Program

Give us a referral who becomes a new customer and we'll pay you $20 or give you a $20 credit on your next bill.

40

Direct Mail Horror Stories

You can use this to…
1. Weigh carefully if direct mail is for you.
2. Save thousands of dollars in unnecessary expenses.

Doing our Cold Calling for Cowards® seminars we sent over two million brochures every year using direct mail. It was our most successful marketing program. (Cold calling seminars using direct mail? Ironic, huh?)

But this book is all about how to get in front of customers, no matter which method you use. Direct mail is one tool you have.

And yes, we did cold call on companies for our seminars. But because our time and personnel were limited, we couldn't call on two million companies each year. We called only on the largest companies while the smaller companies received the brochures.

Would I recommend direct mail for you? I don't know. I don't know what your business or product is. I'd have to know more.

This.

> – Elementary student's answer
> to the test question, "Write an
> example of a risk"

Shooting from the hip, my gut reaction when people ask if they should use direct mail is to say "no". It's risky if you don't know what you're doing or if you're not a large corporation with deep pockets that can afford the gamble.

Do your homework. The rule of thumb that you'll get a 2% response rate on direct mail is baloney. There is no predictor. We would get anywhere from .8% - 1.2% response depending upon the cities we were going to. For us that was worth the investment. But we worked our way into direct mail marketing by taking baby steps (after our first disaster!), by making mistakes that wouldn't bankrupt us, and then finding ways to eliminate those mistakes before taking the next big step.

Think about it. If you could get a 2% response from a mailing, don't you think everyone would be doing it? Even Capital One cut back on their direct mail years ago because of their return rate. They reported they sent 60 billion pieces per year, got at best a .1% response rate, and concluded this was insufficient to justify the enormous expense.

Our first large direct mailing was a heart-stopping horror story and nearly cost us our business right out of the gate. We literally bet our house on the mailings because we took a second mortgage out to pay for them.

The company responsible for the labels gave our Seattle labels to the printer to send to Phoenix and the Phoenix ones to send to Seattle. We didn't discover this until we started getting calls from Phoenix saying they'd like to attend the seminar, but flying to Seattle was out of the question. Holy crap!

Thankfully, the president of the label company admitted their mistake, took full responsibility, covered all our costs, and the thousands of mailings were re-sent getting us the responses we expected.

I'm not an expert on direct mail, but I do have years of experience with it. Your results depend upon several factors: the uniqueness of your service or product, your list of names, how well written and designed your marketing piece is, and the timing of what you're doing.

If you have a service or product no one wants, I don't care how good the mail piece is, it won't sell. Or (speaking from another costly experience) if you have a bad list of names, you can easily lose tens of thousands of dollars on your mailings. You really, really, really have to closely monitor every list on every mailing and keep refining it for the next mailing.

Several speakers who wanted to go into the seminar business like us tried to copy what we did. One friend in California sent out 150,000 direct mail pieces after I advised him against it because of his seminar topic and his market. A total of eleven people signed up for the $100 seminar out of four cities.

Another speaker in New York asked if I would evaluate his brochure and tell him what I thought. After reviewing it, I told him not to send it and suggested several major revisions. He disregarded my suggestions and sent 80,000 pieces to the Boston area (one of our very best cities where we'd get hundreds of attendees each year). He got five sign-ups for his $89 seminar.

Direct mail is a gamble. It takes trial and error, deep pockets, hard work – and a lot of faith. (That, and listen to someone who's paid the cost for the experience.)

41

Hook, Line and Speaker

You can use this to…

1. Get customers' decision makers to come to you.
2. Turn prospects into customers.
3. Increase customer retention and encourage customer feedback.
4. Get referrals from existing customers.
5. Save time; it's like having one sales call on multiple decision makers at once.
6. Build relationships between your management team and your customers' executives.
7. Introduce new services and products.
8. Give salespeople an "excuse" to network and cold call more often.

Here is a business development strategy that "sells" your company and your people, the first thing customers buy, before they'd ever consider your services and products.

This program will find new customers and keep the ones you have. It literally gets your prospects and customers to come to you. It's like making dozens of sales calls on the decision makers on one appointment.

If you're looking to complement to your marketing, networking, cold calling, and customer retention strategies, this is it. Not only does it get all your salespeople involved, but your management as well. I learned this when working for McCaw Communications and it was very successful every time we did it. Here is how you can do your own.

> *Luge strategy? Lie flat and try not to die.*
>
> – Tim Steeves

First, you need a "hook" to draw the crowd. The hook is strictly entertainment for your attendees. If your decision makers are executives, business owners, principals, and top management you want entertainment that will appeal to them. If your decision makers are service, technical or administrative personnel, your entertainment should appeal to them.

The entertainment (the "bait") can be anything from business guest speakers to authors to chefs to magicians to comedians who can tie-in their "spiel" with business. But their presentation cannot be related to your company or your products. Just general business information that your guests can use and take back to their staffs. Their entertainment is to last thirty to sixty minutes, no longer.

The second portion of your program is a presentation by your company's top executives (CEO, president, general manager) on your company, services, and products. This is the opportunity to introduce your top management, meet your customers' executives, and allow your customers to network with their peers. Your presentation should also be thirty to sixty minutes.

Make this a special event requesting R.S.V.P. reservations (the "line"). Let your invitees know this is an opportunity to meet their peers and exchange contact information. Keep your contacts apprised of the names of people and companies that will be attending to motivate them to reserve their space early.

Let your invitees know that you may be introducing new services and products at the end of the meeting, but that no one will be asked to buy anything – in fact, nothing will be sold at this meeting. That is your salespeople's job the week following.

Send invitations to principals, presidents, vice-presidents, executives, general managers, directors, middle managers, supervisors, and business owners. Include a mixture of current customers and prospects. Why prospects? Because your customers will become your best salespeople as they'll talk you up to others in attendance.

Having a program like this encourages your salespeople to call on their existing customers as well as to cold call and network to hand out invitations.

You can hold the event at your company's location or rent a meeting room or ballroom at any local hotel or convention center. Plan on doing at least one event every quarter and inviting different customers and prospects each time.

A variation of this: if you do trade shows use a mini-event like this in the evening as part of your breakout sessions and hand out R.S.V.P. invitations to every guest who stops by your booth.

42

If You Could See Into the Unknown, Would You Go? Do You Have a Choice?

The owner of the last company I worked for before starting my own business over twenty years ago made a comment that surprised me. When I told her that I wanted to leave and start doing seminars (for which I had zero experience, zero knowledge about, and zero financing for), she was behind me 100%.

"That's one thing I've always admired about you," she said. "If there is one word I can use to describe you, it's 'courage'. You'll do things that no one else would ever attempt."

I didn't know what to say. Courage? I didn't know what she was talking about. I never considered myself a person of courage.

I've done a number of things that many of my co-workers, friends or family would never do. Nothing dangerous. Just different. Often uncomfortable. Unusual sometimes.

Her use of the word courage confused me until I finally understood what she meant: I could will myself to take that first step into the unknown with the confidence that I could handle whatever happened.

But to me, it's more about curiosity than courage. I'm always curious about what's around the next bend. I'm always asking the question "How?" How do you do what you do? How does it work? How can I do something others can't do, or they don't think I can do? What is something new that I've never tried before and what can I learn from it?

I've never been afraid of failing; that's a part of being curious. You can't fail when you're curious because you don't know what's supposed to happen. Maybe when you do things out of curiosity it appears you're acting out of courage? I don't know.

> *Many live in dread of what is coming.*
> *Why should we? The unknown puts ad-*
> *venture into life. The unexpected*
> *around the corner gives a sense of an-*
> *ticipation and surprise. Thank God for*
> *the unknown future.*
> — E. Stanley Jones

Curiosity fuels courage. When I got my first professional sales job out of college selling school pictures in Dallas, Texas, I closed the deal without even knowing what a close was until the franchise owner told me a year later. After a brief first interview, I knew I wanted the job but didn't know if the owner was interested in me. I was curious. As I got up I asked him, "I'm interested in you. Are you interested in me?"

The owner told me that's why I got the job over the other two finalists who had better résumés than me. He said it took courage to ask him for the job after only the first interview. My curiosity gave me the courage to ask.

If you don't think you can get the courage to cold call, why not become curious about who your prospects are doing business with?

That's what my school picture boss taught me about cold calling. He said it would take three years before my sales would take off. The principals had to see me coming back year after year before they would trust me enough to give me their business. So he told me to make my cold calls all about finding out who was taking their school's pictures. It worked. And my sales took off like a skyrocket in the thirty-fifth month, just like he said.

Starting to work with McCaw, I adopted the same strategy. I was making fifty to seventy walk-in cold calls a day. I'd walk in to a company and, without even introducing myself, say, "I was talking with your neighbors next door about our pagers. Just wanted to stop by and see who you're doing business with."

I made those calls because I was curious. I led the nation every year for our company in new business found through cold calling, and it was my curiosity that helped me to find them.

Dr. Viktor Frankl's concept of paradoxical intention mentioned earlier got my curiosity. Can you really create courage by being a coward? Our seminar attendees will swear to it. That's why I registered the name of the program Cold Calling for Cowards®.

Curiosity and courage are intertwined somehow. I'm just not for sure how.

When you're networking or working trade shows, be curious about everyone you meet. Ask them about their business. Ask them how they got started. Ask them how they find customers. Ask them for the best and worst advice they can give you about selling.

If you read something in this book or other books, be curious: "Will this work for me?" Then give it a shot.

In Joe Girard's book *How to Sell Anything to Anybody* he had a referral program that he said worked for him. I was curious. Would it work for me? I tried it. It worked. I also led the nation for McCaw every year in referrals because of his idea. It didn't take courage. Only curiosity to see if I could duplicate it.

Maxwell Maltz (*Psycho-Cybernetics*), Og Mandino (*The Greatest Salesman in the World*), and Frank Bettger (*How I Raised Myself from Failure to Success in Selling*) all referred back to a technique by Ben Franklin for how to create habits. Mandino said that if you would follow the plan in his book for one year that you would triple your income in that year. I was curious: could I do this for a year? And could I triple my income? I did and I did.

What's finding new business all about? Courage and curiosity. They're easy to get. Courage by taking that first step. Curiosity by trying something new. You're lucky. They're both on the same exciting path.

> *Two roads diverged in a wood, and I—*
> *I took the one less traveled by,*
> *And that has made all the difference.*
> – Robert Frost, "The Road Not Taken"

Bonus

Remembering Names

It's Not Magic
If You Know How It's Done

Jerry Hocutt

Introduction

Dr. Majid Fotuhi, a neurologist and memory expert at Johns Hopkins, said that "The number one memory complaint people have is that they're bad with names."

Memory expert Harry Lorayne said that "One of the highest rated talents you can have in business is the ability to remember names."

The best piece of advice I ever got when getting into the speaking business over twenty years ago was from another speaker, Bob Burg. It applies to everyone who has contact with people whether you're a businessperson, salesperson, teacher, preacher, military commander, coach, or medical professional.

Bob said learn how to remember people's names. He said it's weird. People look at you like you're performing magic. The most valuable people skill you will probably ever develop is learning how to remember names. Other than giving someone your winning Powerball lotto ticket, it's one of the fastest ways to impress and influence others.

I've done hundreds of sales presentations, just not on the subject of remembering names. Trying to remember names is a hobby I have. We may have a group of 200-500 participants in each program and I'll call on a number of them by their names throughout the session. I'm always surprised that after every program people ask, "How do you remember so many names?"

Let's be clear: I'm not a name savant. I can't hold a candle to the likes of Benjamin Levy and Harry Lorayne and remember 300 names in a room. I just remember the ones I call on during the programs – maybe 20-30 attendees. Like you I have to work at it. I forget names like anyone else. Just ask my wife of 48 years, uh, uh…her name's on the tip of my tongue.

The good news is you'll never have to remember the names of a roomful of people either unless you have an act that calls for it. But you will need to remember a few names as you move through life. Here are some of the things I've learned that always work. They'll work for you too.

Hey! I Remember You...I Just Don't Remember Your Name

Let me illustrate the basic concept for how to remember names. In Netflix's *House of Cards*, what is the character's name that Kevin Spacey plays? In the TV comedy, *The Middle*, what is the character's name that Atticus Shaffer plays (the youngest son)? Claire Danes plays the CIA agent in Netflix's *Homeland*. What is her character's name? (Answers: Frank Underwood, Brick Heck, Carrie Mathison.)

I gave you two hooks to remember their names: the names of the shows and the names of the stars.

And that's the basic concept for how to remember names: find something – *anything* – to remind you of the name. Just like a nametag, you're looking for a hook.

If you want to have your own stage act of remembering names, two books I highly recommend are *Remember Every Name Every Time* by Benjamin Levy, and *Amazing Face Reading* by Mac Fulfer. Fulfer is a Ft. Worth attorney and jury consultant. You may not agree with his ideas on reading faces, but his book is excellent because you learn how to look at faces in a new way. He has ten pages and drawings on the eyes alone. Nine pages on the nose.

Where to start

For those of you who used CliffsNotes and Wikipedia as your sources of information in school so you wouldn't get bogged down with having to actually read the entire assignment, here's *HocuttsShortcuts* for how to remember names. Details follow.

1. Know when to **listen** for the name.
2. **Hear** the name. This is the *number one reason* you don't remember names: you never heard it to begin with.
3. **Spell** the name silently to yourself.
4. **Look** at the face. Really look at it. Men, don't be looking around the room trying to find the nearest exit. And women, don't look down to see if the men's shoes match.
5. Pick out the first **feature** on their face that jumps out at you. (Where Fulfer's book is invaluable.) It could be the color of their eyes, the shape of their eyebrows, their nose, their ears, their chin. It doesn't make any difference. This is going to be your "hook". It's like a biological nametag stuck to their face. Every time you see that hook, it's going to remind you of the name.
6. **Tie-in** the name with the hook. Make the tie-in as silly or as outrageous as possible.

Know when to *listen* for the name

If I'm meeting someone new, my radar goes up the minute we shake hands. I don't want to be distracted by looking around the room or thinking about what I'm going to say.

If I'm meeting someone and shaking hands and I didn't hear their name I'll hold the handshake a beat longer, take a step closer in and say, "I'm sorry. I didn't catch your name. Could you repeat that?" No one has ever been offended. In fact, they're pleased that you want to get their name right.

If it is an unusual *first* name I'll say something like, "That's a name I haven't heard before. Is that a family name? How did you get it? How do you spell it?" Again, no one is offended.

A great place to practice knowing *when* to listen for names is when you're on the phone. When someone calls you, or you call someone's office, listen for the names of everyone you connect with. Write the name down. Keep your pen in your hand as a *reminder* to listen for the name.

Another place to practice when to listen is when you go to a restaurant and the waiter comes to take your order. As you're handed the menu, the waiter will slip in his name. You're expecting it. Grab it. To reinforce your memory, thank him by using his name when he says "I'll be right back to take your order"; and then use his name again when he brings the check.

Next, *hear* the name

Harry Lorayne says that doing this one thing – hearing the name – will get you to **remember 50% more of the people** you meet because you *have* to pay attention. And for most business and social situations remembering the first name is good enough.

If I should forget their name later I'll admit it. I'll tell them, "I'm sorry; my mind just left me without telling me it was going. Could you give me your name again?"

Spell the name

The third thing on our list is to spell the name silently to yourself. Spelling it gives you another hook to remember.

You don't need to spell it correctly. Grades will not be given. Use "texting shorthand" and spell it like you're texting a friend; leave out the vowels if you want. All we're looking for is a *reminder* of the name – not the correct spelling.

If you're meeting a room full of people, you'll have to skip this step because you won't have time. But if it's just two or three people, spell it.

I've even found another shortcut for spelling the name that's quick and fun. Years ago I learned the American Sign Language alphabet. Now when I meet someone I'll use the sign of just one of the letters in their name that stands out. For example, I'll use the "x" for Max, "z" for Zoe, "l" for Lisa, "v" for David, "t" for Natalie, "g" for Regina. You get the picture. Making that one signing letter makes me pay attention to that person and pay attention to the letter I chose. That alone is usually enough for me to remember the name. Download any free sign language app and learn them. They're easy. Did I mention fun?

Look at the face

Don't worry that people will think you're staring at them. Benjamin Levy tells of a study of two groups conducting conversations. The first group was told to carry on a normal conversation. No special instructions were given. The second group was told to count the number of blinks of the other person while they were talking. The researchers found that the people who were having their blinks counted felt more positive toward the listeners because they felt they were paying more attention to what they were saying. Looking at the face leads you to the next step.

Select a facial feature

Pick out a feature on the face that stands out. They don't have to have the two heads like Dot and Bette Tattler in *American Horror Story* or the Cyclops eye of Stuart the Minion in *Despicable Me*. Just gravitate to the first thing that gets your attention. It could be the eyes, the ears, the nose, the lips. Maybe it's a mole or lines on the face. It doesn't make any difference.

The feature you pick is your "hook" to remind you of their name. Every time you see that feature – their biological nametag – it should remind you of their name.

Let's go to work

Here's a picture of Robin, the president of her company. What features jump out at you?

Some that get my attention are the...

1. Heavy eyelids
2. Winged eyebrows
3. High cheek bones
4. Cupid's bow upper lip

Now tie-in Robin's name with the feature you choose. When I look at that feature – my hook – I want it to remind me of Robin's name.

With Robin I'm going with the eyelids, especially her left eyelid which is larger. Instead of an eyelid, I see a robin's bird nest. The nest is so heavy that it's forcing her left eye shut – in fact, making her wink flirtatiously at me. Now every time I look at Robin, the first thing I'll notice is her left eyelid and I'll see the robin's nest as she's winking at me. I just have to make sure I don't wink back.

Make silly pictures. Make them humongous. Make them tiny. Maybe see hundreds of birds' nests on her eyelid. If you can put them in motion, even better.

Next, let's meet Robin's vice president, Tony.
What I see…
1. Thick eye-brows
2. Broad chin
3. Perfect teeth
4. Lines under his eyes

I'm going with the thick eyebrows. I have a nephew whose name is Tony. There's also Tony the Tiger. The picture I see is my nephew ripping off one of Tony's eyebrows and Tony the Tiger ripping off the other. Tony screams from the pain. Blood is pulsing out from where his eyebrows were. My two Tony's are sword fighting using Tony's eyebrows. Silly, graphic, in motion and memorable.

The last person in the meeting is Robin's general manager, B.D. Driscoll (next page). He only goes by his initials, B.D.
Three things that stick out are…
1. High forehead
2. Very thin upper lip
3. Ears are flat against his head

Since B.D. is going to make it hard for me by not having a first name, I'm going to make him pay for it. I'm going to use a hot branding iron and brand "BD" on his forehead for "bad decision" for not having a first name. Of course, he's going to scream in pain because the branding iron was just pulled from the campfire. The BD on his forehead is now pulsating and glowing like a red neon sign.

So there you have it: Robin, Tony, and B.D. Believe it or not, making these pictures only takes a few seconds. You'll usually have both the name and the picture in your mind before you finish shaking hands with each of the three.

Now let's put it altogether with three simple exercises.

Fun Xercises

Use these three exercises to help improve your observational skills and remember names better.

Exercise 1

For one week watch anything on TV: the news, movies, regular programs. Look at the faces. Don't try to name or label any of the features. Your objective is to simply observe.

Look at their eyes. Do the corners of their eyes angle up like Angelina Jolie's, or angle down like Russell Crowe's? Do their ears protrude like President Barack Obama's, or do they look like they're stapled flat to their head like Bill Kristol's? Is their nose crooked like NBC's Brian Williams, or is it large and bulbous like Bill Clinton's?

The next week watch any TV program. Pick out a feature on each face and tie-in their name with the feature.

For Frank Underwood's character in *House of Cards* I see giant, hairy, frankfurters as his eyebrows. For Brick Heck in *The Middle* I see his protruding ears as gigantic bricks that keep slamming against the sides of his head.

Exercise 2

This exercise is easy, easy, easy. When you're checking out at the grocery store, getting your burger at a fast food joint, or giving the barista your order, look at the clerk's nametag. Look at the face. Match the name with the feature you've selected. Then, as they're handing you the receipt or your order, call them by their name.

You'll be surprised by the reaction – and better service – you get when you call people by their name. They're flattered that you would think they're important enough to learn their name. After all, how does it make you feel when someone calls you by your name? (Unless it's the SWAT team or the IRS.)

Exercise 3

At work, look at your co-workers and pick one feature that stands out. Name it: chin, eyes, nose, lips, ears?

Tie-in their name with the feature you selected. If Ernie has small ears, I'd find a word that *sounds* like Ernie: burning. When I see Ernie's small ears I'm thinking, "His ears are burning and getting so small."

If Olivia has large blue eyes I'd see them as olives and say, "I've never seen blue olives before."

If her name is Lady Gaga, I'd say...well, what can you say? That's just weird.

The words and pictures you choose don't have to be identical to the person's name. The mind's natural memory will make the correct association between the *feature* you choose, the *word* you use, and that person's *name*. Remember, all you're looking for is a reminder, a hook.

Each day get better at hearing the names. Get better at looking at faces. Get better at selecting features. Get better at coming up with silly associations.

If you're like me you may never master remembering the names of everyone you meet. But you *can* get better at it. It's a valuable skill. People will be impressed. And you will be too.

I can remember names and faces better because I *want* to do it. So can you.

About the Author

Jerry Hocutt is a Seattle author, speaker, and sales trainer. He was the #1 salesman in the nation for a Fortune 1000 company for three years. He's trained over 150,000 salespeople, executives, managers, business owners, entrepreneurs, and professionals from thousands of companies across America in his nationally acclaimed Cold Calling for Cowards® seminars.

Some of thousands of companies that have attended his seminars include...

Bank of America · Coldwell Banker · UPS · FedEx · Verizon · Nextel Sprint · IBM · Xerox · ADP · Merrill Lynch · Hyatt · GE · SBC Communications · Morgan Stanley · Office Depot · Dell · State Farm · Marriott · Ritz-Carlton · Farmers · AFLAC · Avaya · U.S. Marines · Clear Channel · Chicago Title · Los Angeles Times · Key Bank · St. Petersburg Times · Wells Fargo Bank · U.S. Bank · Gallup · Westin Hotels · Allstate · Hilton Hotels · New York Life · Xpedx · Adecco Staffing · LaSalle Bank · Boeing · Aramark · Pfizer Staples · Toastmasters · Sir Speedy · Kelly Services · CB Richard Ellis · Edward Jones · Kinko's · Manpower · Minuteman Press · Safeco · Ameriprise · Staubach · Dale Carnegie · Condé Nast · Forest Lawn

> Hocutt's paying audience knows the truth: Calling strangers for a living can be hell. They are the foot soldiers in America's business-to-business selling game. And Hocutt is their drill sergeant. His plain-spokeness wins people over.
> *– Los Angeles Times, "He's the Zen Master of Cold Calls"*

> Hocutt certainly can ease the pain from perhaps one of the most dreaded duties in the business world: the cold call.
> *– New Jersey Star-Ledger, "The Lord of the Rings"*

Titles by Jerry Hocutt

Paperbacks and eBooks

Cold Calling Is Like a Colonoscopy without the Drugs – How You Can Find New Business with Courage, Cold Calling and a Few Less Invasive Techniques

Cold Calling for Cowards® – How to Turn the Fear of Rejection into Opportunities, Sales, and Money

The Wickedly Fun Dictionary of Business – Words That Escaped Me Before My Brain Finished Downloading

The Book on Sales Tips - one tip, one page, one minute

eBooks Only

The Blueprint for Cold Calling Scripts – What to Say, How to Say It, and Why You Say It

Cold Calling Works? Prove It! – How to Want to Do What You Hate to Do When You Need to Do It

Cast in Stone – 45 Sales Fundamentals That Should Never Be Tampered With

Selling Doesn't Always Have to Be a Struggle – 45 Ways to Put the Fun Back Into Selling

Selling Doesn't Come With Instructions – 45 Ways to Put It Together

Sales Psych – 45 Sales Motivation Tips for Tough Times

Sales Calls Are Auditions – 45 Ways to Get a Callback

Free PDF eBooks available only at www.FootInTheDoor.com

Lunch? – 20 Sales Questions I've Been Asked Over Lunch

Remembering Names – It's Not Magic If You Know How It's Done

The Wickedly Fun Dictionary of Business – Words That Escaped Me Before My Brain Finished Downloading (abridged edition)